Contents

Acknowledgements

We are grateful to the following for permission to reproduce copyright material:

Cambridge University Press for an extract from pp 101–104 *Unemployment* by P Kelvin & J Jarrett (pub CUP 1985); Macmillan Accounts and Administration for extracts from pp xiii & 32 *The Nature of Work* by P Thompson (pub Macmillan 1983); Open University Educational Enterprises Ltd for extracts from pp 100–101, 155–159, 174–175 *Education, Unemployment and The Future of Work* by A Watts (pub Open Univ Press 1983); Pluto Press for an extract from pp 112–121 *Brothers: Male Dominance and Technological Change* by C Cockburn (pub Pluto Press 1985) Copyright (c) 1985 Cynthia Cockburn; University of California Press for extracts from pp 524–538 *Social Problems* Vol 26 No 5, June 1979 (c) 1979 by The Society For The Study of Social Problems.

For Delia and Alison – who help me put the phrase 'learning to labour' into perspective – and Herbert, who did everything he could to prevent me from finishing this book.

I would like to thank Rowena Gay for typing Part 3 of the manuscript.

TFLEPEN

SOCIOLOGY IN
General Editor: Murray Morison

This book is to be returned on
or before the date stamped below

LONGMAN GROUP UK LIMITED
*Longman House, Burnt Mill, Harlow, Essex CM20 2JE, UK
and Associated Companies throughout the World.*

**Published in the United States of America
by Longman Inc., New York.**

© **Longman Group UK Limited 1987**
*All rights reserved; no part of this publication
may be reproduced, stored in a retrieval system,
or transmitted in any form or by any means, electronic,
mechanical, photocopying, recording, or otherwise,
without the prior written permission of the Publishers.*

*First published 1987
ISBN 0 582 35499 4*

Set in 10/11pt Bembo, Linotron 202

***Produced by Longman Group (FE) Ltd
Printed in Hong Kong***

British Library Cataloguing in Publication Data
Horne, John
  Work, employment and unemployment. −
  (Sociology in focus series).
  1. Industrial sociology
  I. Title II. Series
  306′.36 HD6955
  ISBN 0-582-35499-4

Library of Congress Cataloging in Publication Data

Horne, John (John D.)
  Work, employment and unemployment.

  (Sociology in focus series)
  Bibliography: p.
  Includes index.
  Summary: Identifies the theories, trends, and
issues of work and unemployment and discusses the
relationship between sociology and work.
  1. Work. 2. Unemployment. (1. Work. 2. Unemploy-
ment) I. Title. II. Series.
HD4901.H66 1988   306′.36   87-3671
ISBN 0-582-35499-4 (pbk.)

Series introduction

Sociology in Focus aims to provide an up-to-date, coherent coverage of the main topics that arise on an introductory course in sociology. While the intention is to do justice to the intricacy and complexity of current issues in sociology, the style of writing has deliberately been kept simple. This is to ensure that the student coming to these ideas for the first time need not become lost in what can appear initially as jargon.

Each book in the series is designed to show something of the purpose of sociology and the craft of the sociologist. Throughout the different topic areas the interplay of theory, methodology and social policy have been highlighted, so that rather than sociology appearing as an unwieldy collection of facts, the student will be able to grasp something of the process whereby sociological understanding is developed. The format of the books is broadly the same throughout. Part one provides an overview of the topic as a whole. In part two the relevant research is set in the context of the theoretical, methodological and policy issues. The student is encouraged to make his or her own assessment of the various arguments, drawing on the statistical and reference material provided both here and at the end of the book. The final part of the book contains both statistical material and a number of 'Readings'. Questions have been provided in this section to direct students to analyse the materials presented in terms of both theoretical assumptions and methodological approaches. It is intended that this format should enable students to exercise their own sociological imaginations rather than to see sociology as a collection of universally accepted facts, which just have to be learned.

While each book in the series is complete within itself, the similarity of format ensures that the series as a whole provides an integrated and balanced introduction to sociology. It is intended that the text can be used both for individual and classroom study, while the inclusion of the variety of statistical and documentary materials lend themselves to both the preparation of essays and brief seminars.

PART 1

Introduction and overview

1 Changes at work

Introduction

This short topic book aims to review recent sociological writing on work, employment and unemployment. Sociological research and writing always develops under specific social conditions. Theories, perspectives and issues for research are fashioned and altered as the 'real world' changes. In the current social climate of mass unemployment, occupational shifts and economic restructuring, the study of work has been particularly subject to change. As Professor Richard Brown has noted: 'The predominant characteristics of employment in the early 1960s and what was problematic about work then, are no longer an adequate agenda for research work in the 1980s' (in Thompson (ed.), *Work, Employment and Unemployment*, Open University Press, 1984). Fundamental social institutions, structures and processes have become questioned as the crisis has made its impact felt in the advanced capitalist countries. Britain, as the first industrial nation, has perhaps been transformed the most, with a massive decline in manufacturing employment and the re-emergence of unemployment rates in some parts of the country which are worse than those of the 1930s. Such developments (which I shall look at in more detail in the next chapter) have fuelled debates about the very meaning of work in contemporary society.

Supporters of the new technology (micro-electronics and robotics) point to a potential for increasing the opportunities for leisure. They see in new technology the opportunity to counter boredom and alienation at work, as the amount of work to be done diminishes. Others point to the tediousness and toil of many jobs which will remain untouched by new technology, the poor rewards and insecurity of work in an economic system which places production for profit as the primary goal. They see in the technological revolution yet another chapter in the history of capitalist exploitation and control of the workforce. Last, but not least, the contemporary women's movement has drawn attention to the vast amount of unpaid, and hence largely neglected, low-status labour carried out mainly by women in the domestic sphere. Nor has the fact that legislation in the 1970s has failed to produce little real equality at work between the sexes escaped the attention of commentators a decade later.

Contemporary sociological theorising and research into work is being influenced by this social climate. There has always been a healthy scepticism about the simple equation of 'work' with paid employment. Yet in wider society the prevailing meaning of the word is just that: so, 'an active woman, running a house and bringing up children, is distinguished from a woman who works: that is to say, takes paid employment' (R. Williams, *Keywords*, Fontana, 1983, p. 335).

Sociologists have long been aware that *wage-labour*, to give its technical name, is only a particular form of work, gaining its centrality and definition from the specific set of productive relations which occurs within capitalist, market-exchange economies. Work, in such societies, is identified with *employment*, which involves 'the sale and purchase of labour power as a commodity in a market, resulting in the direction of activity during "working hours" by persons who have acquired the right to do so by virtue of the labour contract' (K. Purcell, 'Work, employment and unemployment', in R. G. Burgess (ed.), *Key Variables in Social Investigation*, Routledge & Kegan Paul, 1986, p. 155). If sociologists have recognised this generally, its significance has usually been disregarded when the study of work has begun in earnest. The focus has predominantly been on employment, in factories (rarely offices), and on male workers. This emphasis is now being challenged as a result of the decline in employment, the arguments of feminists, and the growing awareness of other forms of work 'outside employment'. Just as (paid) work is apparently contracting, social scientific interest in it appears to be higher than ever. One sign is the launch of two new journals in 1986/1987: *New Technology, Work and Employment* and *Work, Employment and Society*. Sociologists have been forced to consider unemployment, work outside the 'formal' economy, and the way in which the domains of the public and private (paid work and unpaid, domestic work) are related. Much of this research is at a very early stage, and is only just gaining momentum. It will not be possible to provide a guide to all the strands in the new thinking on work in this book. But a few brief remarks about recent areas of interest seem appropriate at this stage.

Work outside employment

Western governments have recently begun to assess the amount of work that takes place in the *black* or 'informal' economy. Increasingly, sociologists have come to see that the study of formal employment does not exhaust the scope of the sociology of work. Sociologist **Ray Pahl** and economist **Jonathan Gershuny** published a provocative article in *New Society* (3 Jan. 1980) entitled 'Britain in the decade of the three economies', in which they put forward the idea that there were in fact three different economies within which people work – the formal, the informal and the household. In the formal economy, the one recognised by governments, people sell their ability to labour for wages and salaries; in the informal economy people might do work 'off the books' – that is, receive cash but not declare it to the state (the real 'black economy') or they might do a job for a neighbour or relative which would be repaid 'in kind'; in the household economy Pahl and Gershuny gave prominence to the role of women in performing routine cooking, cleaning and caring in the home, as well as 'do-it-yourself' self-service work carried out by both men and women. The actual detail of their argument need not concern us. Pahl has written that he no longer agrees with his 1980 conclusions. The interesting thing about the article was the attempt to account systematically for a wider range of activities that could be termed 'work' than social scientists had done conventionally. Everyone knows, without doing sociology courses, that a great deal of work gets done which is not recorded in official statistics or sociological surveys. Here was a suggestion as to how researchers might go about locating this work and analysing its significance in society.

Since 1980 conferences have been held, research has flourished and books and articles have been published on activities 'outside

Table 1.1   *Different types of work and economy*

Paid	Unpaid
Wage-labour in the formal economy	Domestic labour in the household economy
Shadow wage-labour in the black economy	Work outside employment in the communal economy

employment'. The table above summarises different types of work and economy that have been identified by researchers.

A useful way of clarifying the differences, which we can borrow from Pahl's book *Divisions of Labour* (Basil Blackwell, 1984), is to imagine a woman ironing a garment at home. She could be ironing a garment before she delivers it to her employer for wages as an 'outworker' (wage-labour in the formal economy). She could be ironing a garment which she proposes to sell to get some extra cash without declaring it to the state (wage-labour or self-employment in the 'black economy'). She might be ironing a garment as a housewife for her husband upon whom she is financially dependent (domestic labour in the 'household economy'). Or, finally, she could be ironing a garment, with no expectation of payment, for a friend, neighbour or relative, or out of some obligation to the local church, club or other voluntary organisation to which she belongs (work outside of employment in the 'communal economy'). Perhaps you can think of some additional explanations for the woman's actions, related to different economies?

The unemployed and the 'black economy'

In a recent article Ray Pahl has remarked that 'anecdote too often serves as a substitute for more substantial empirical evidence' in the debate about the nature of work outside employment (in 'The politics of work', *The Political Quarterly*, Oct.–Dec. 1985). This is especially the case with the unemployed. For example, a *Times* editorial in March 1985 concluded: 'Everyone of us knows from our own experience that there is a huge unofficial economy at work, much of it concentrated in the labour market where it makes a mockery of the raw unemployment figures. Many of those people who are on the dole are in part-time work and we all know it' (29 March 1985). But, despite this assertion, there is no hard evidence that what 'we all know' is in fact the case. Indeed, as Pahl makes clear, most research evidence available, including his own, suggests that the unemployed are actually *less* likely to engage in *any* informal work outside the home, whether or not it is paid, and, for men at least, they are 'also less likely to do domestic work inside the home than are those in full time employment'. Counter-intuitive this information may be, but that is why we do social science research, Things are not always what they seem! At the same time it is not difficult to see that a general belief that the black economy somehow offsets the burden of unemployment is a comfort for any government presiding over such high rates of it. Despite this there are several reasons why the unemployed are less likely to work 'off the books': a person used to regular paid work for twenty years or so who is made redundant is unprepared for the world of 'quick-footed informal entrepreneuring'; the unemployed tend to lack social and physical means of access to informal work opportunities (they are unable to run a car or van, are less likely to have a telephone, cannot afford to go to pubs, and are often geographically isolated); and recent studies suggest that the unemployed are quite likely to be informed on to the authorities if they are believed to be working. In short, Pahl concludes from his research that it is those already in employment who may be in the best position to take advantage of various fiddles and perks.

The division of labour

While much of the sociology of work consists of research into men at work in factories, often with the assumption that their experience is 'authentic' work, typical of and generalisable to other groups of workers, in the last fifteen years this view has been challenged. Feminist perspectives in industrial sociology, labour economics and women's studies have pointed to the 'invisibility of women' in conventional research. A good example of the feminist critique is the article by Professor **Margaret Stacey**, 'The Division of Labour Revisited or Overcoming the Two Adams' (in P. Abrams *et al.* (eds), *Practice and Progress: British Sociology 1950–1980*, Allen & Unwin, 1981). Stacey argues that

the key concepts of the 'founding fathers' of sociology and economics in the eighteenth and especially the nineteenth centuries
were largely developed for understanding *paid employment* in the
capitalist labour market and the actions of men in the 'public'
arena of the state. As such, 'work', in sociology as in the rest of
society, has tended to be equated almost solely with paid employment. Only work which is remunerated through the 'cash nexus',
through market-place transactions and is counted and taxed by
government has been seen as 'real work'.

Attention has been focused on paid work, as a key variable in
sociological research, because there is a strong relationship
between a person's occupation, his or her rewards from work and
his or her social class or status. However, as Stacey argues, this
focus on paid work and the refinement of concepts to understand
its importance has meant that the study of the 'private' realms of
family and kin and the relationship between the 'public' and the
'private', the 'economic' and the 'gender' order, have always been
secondary in sociology. This has helped sustain a 'male' view of
the social world and led to the general neglect of other forms of
work which take place outside of the formal economic system.
The feminist economist Anne Phillips supports this view: 'The
activities that can dominate women's lives – looking after children, caring for sick relatives, shopping, cleaning, washing,
cooking – none of these will figure in the "economy". Under
capitalism we only really count things when money changes
hands' (*Hidden Hands*, Pluto Press, 1982). The feminist critique
has made sociologists aware of the need to think again about their
conceptualisation of work and the division of labour in society.

The argument of the book

Here, then, we can see a clear connection between social change
and sociological theory and research. Sociologists interested in the
study of work have been caught up in public debates and have
been forced to reconsider some fundamental assumptions. But one
of our central aims is to enable you to cut through the confusion
by critically examining some of the contemporary views about
work, employment and unemployment. In our opinion sociologists need to be wary of statements about 'the collapse of work',
'the flight from work' or the possibility of 'liberation from work'

(these are recent book titles). No matter how superficially appealing or attractive, we need to avoid what Michael Young once described as 'the tyranny of an imagined future over the present'. Two themes in particular underpin the argument of this book. Firstly, paid employment, or *wage-labour*, remains, and will continue to be, a fundamental determinant of people's lives, and secondly, the actual *experience* of work has to be seen as the product of social relations such as age and ethnicity and, especially, gender.

Paid work is the central mechanism for the distribution of economic rewards *and* deprivation. It is the single most important determinant of people's *life chances*. This is so because we continue to live in a capitalist market economy. Labour is treated as a commodity – a service or good that can be bought and sold – and is used to create other commodities which can then be sold to realise profits. As **Anthony Giddens** writes, although Western societies have changed significantly since the nineteenth century they remain very much capitalist economies in respect of the qualities listed below:

1 production for profit, involving the dominance of privately owned capital, remains the main dynamic impetus of the economic system;
2 ownership of private property, particularly capital ownership, remains highly unequal;
3 class conflict continues to be of primary significance in both the economy and the polity.
(*Sociology – A Brief but Critical Introduction*, Macmillan, 1982, p. 70)

Although there have been important changes in the occupational structure of countries like Britain in this century, we would contend that these have not entailed a fundamental change in the class structure. As Giddens says, these capitalist societies remain 'class societies'. Contemporary social problems, such as unemployment and the existence of forms of 'work outside employment', need to be examined from within this perspective. As Chas Critcher has written: 'That anyone should be allowed to live a materially sufficient and psychologically satisfying existence without exchanging his or her labour for wages is no more acceptable now than it has ever been in the history of industrial capitalism' ('The historical dimension of leisure' in A. Veal *et al.*

(eds), *Work and leisure*, Leisure Studies Association Conference Paper 15, n.d., p. 10).

Research into forms of work previously ignored in the sociology of work – women's paid work, work in the family, and other forms of paid and unpaid work – is now taking place. This research is important because until we know about the work that people actually do, other than that for which they officially receive a wage, then we have no way of assessing claims about the relative contribution of different social groups to the maintenance and reproduction of society. We are also in a poor position to begin to discuss how we might cope with the decline in the amount of time taken up by formal paid employment as a result of 'new technology' if we do not know how 'non-work' time is taken up. This is especially important with respect to women, as it is clear that the home and family are a different experience for them than for men. Socially generated obligations and expectations about male and female roles are important determinants of people's lives. The running of a home is still largely seen as part of a woman's 'duties', despite the growth in women's employment since World War II. Despite over-optimistic speculations in the early 1970s that men and women were increasingly trading conventional family roles and responsibilities, no research since then has confirmed any trend toward the 'symmetrical' family. Likewise, although some research suggests that the 'black economy' has grown during the economic crisis of the last ten years, it is important to keep its size and significance in perspective. In sum, work 'outside' formal employment needs to be studied in relation to that which goes on 'inside'. Researchers need to consider the *interconnections* between the two 'spheres' – if they are conceived like that – and both examine how wage-labour relations penetrate unpaid work, and how socially generated ideologies shape patterns of waged work.

The rest of the book

In Part 2 we will look at some key areas for understanding the world of work, employment and unemployment. In Chapter 2 we will briefly outline the contemporary context within which the sociology of work has developed and look at different explanations of the 'jobs crisis'. Sociological research always proceeds by way of the observation of a subject through the lens of a theory or perspective. Chapter 3 discusses the different theoretical traditions which existed in the sociology of work until fifteen years ago, while Chapter 4 looks at more recent theoretical and empirical work. In Chapter 5 we shall consider sociological research into unemployment. In the concluding chapter we consider the future of work and how the sociology of work may develop.

One of the problems with the 'topic book' format is that space is severely limited. As a result, certain 'conventional' topics – job satisfaction, organisational theory and the professions – are not explicitly covered. A second problem is that complex arguments have, inevitably, to be compressed. Discussions of research can make it look as though the subject never resolves any of the problems which it sets itself. This is partly correct. Much of sociology involves the constant re-evaluation of past theories and suggested ways of looking at the social world in the light of novel conditions and situations. The promise of the topic book, particularly in this format, is that it will whet the reader's appetite for the area of concern and make her or him want to find out more. For this reason we provide full references where research is cited as well as a guide to further reading at the back of the book.

Sociology and work

---

2 Economic change in Britain

In this chapter we shall briefly examine the major features of contemporary economic change in the British economy and their impact on the world of work. Competing perspectives on economic decline will then be introduced and evaluated. The aim is to provide a backdrop for Part 2, where developments in the sociological study of work, employment and unemployment will be outlined and assessed. Three aspects of economic change stand out in modern Britain: the relocation of production, the changes consequently brought about in the occupational structure and the growth of recorded unemployment to unprecedented heights.

Relocating production

What we have now to explain is something quite different [from old-fashioned capitalism]: a world of giant companies not simply trading across the world but producing as well as selling in many countries, moving their capital to develop raw materials in one place, employ cheap labour in another, take advantage of special skills in a third and everywhere standardizing production and consumption to their patterns. . . . When a handful of companies decide what we eat and drink and wear and sing and use for heat or transport or entertainment and how we develop our economies, not only in the capitalist world but in the Soviet Union and Eastern Europe and even in China and Cuba, then we need a new model to explain the working of such gigantic forces.

(From M. Barratt Brown, *Models in Political Economy*, Penguin Books, 1984)

Barratt Brown is referring to the development of capitalism in the twentieth century. As it has become a worldwide economic system, so capital has become concentrated and centralised in larger and larger companies through takeovers and mergers. A few hundred of them have come to dominate the world market. Multinationals – such as the US oil company Exxon (Esso) and the car giant General Motors, Japan's Mitsubishi, the Anglo-Dutch concerns Shell and Unilever, and British-based companies like BP and Blue Circle Cement – have the financial reserves and flexibility to shift their sphere and mode of operation in search of the most profitable returns on investment. They operate on a worldwide basis without allegiance to any one national economy or nation state. Although production takes place throughout the world, decision making is highly centralised. Headquarters – usually in a city such as New York, London, Paris or Tokyo – will have direct control over the other elements of the company. With the developments in transport, telecommunications and information technology in the last twenty years industrial location and control of production have become less and less dependent on geographic distances. A 'new international division of labour' has been made possible. The result is that Western nations generally, and Britain in particular, have become relatively less powerful in the world economic order. Governments of nation states are no longer the only important actors on the world economic stage.

Governments have increasingly intervened in the workings of national economies this century, providing through education, social welfare and policies of economic management, the conditions within which capitalist corporations might flourish. They have also become major employers: over 25 per cent of all employment in Britain by the late 1970s was 'public sector' – that is, national and local government, nationalised industries, the armed forces and so on. But measures employed by the state have not been enough to sustain 'full' or 'near full' employment, and since 1979 Conservative governments have been ideologically opposed to government intervention in the economy. Not surprisingly, the relocation of manufacturing industry in both 'traditional' sectors (such as shipbuilding, textiles and clothing) and 'modern' sectors (for instance, vehicles and electronics) to the Third World – South-east Asia and Latin American countries – has continued. For the multinationals, the ability to relocate production on a global scale and exploit the advantage of doing so – cheaper labour costs, longer working hours, fewer environmental and safety controls and weaker labour organisations – have been too good to miss. While Third World productivity approximates to that in the West, the subdivision and 'de-skilling' of the work processes make them suitable for unskilled, hence cheaper, labour. The company gets the same product for a fraction of the cost (see Reading 8.1, pp. 91–3, for help with these terms).

It would be wrong, however, to think that the relocation of production has only been occurring internationally. Relocation of manufacturing has been taking place within the borders of countries such as the UK and the USA as well. Industrial analysts refer to a geographical reorganisation of the US economy, with a shift from the 'frost belt', in the older industrial regions of the North and East, to the 'sun belt', in the South and West, during the decade between the mid-1960s and mid-1970s. In the UK, when people talk about 'economic decline' it is important to realise that such changes have been very uneven. Although all regions have lost jobs in manufacturing they have done so at different rates. Non-manufacturing changes have also been geographically differentiated. As D. B. Massey and R. A. Meegan wrote in the early 1980s:

> In some cities, and in the South East region, losses in manufacturing have been more than compensated for, in numerical terms at least, by gains in service sector jobs. In some individual towns, however, which have seen the virtual extinction of their manufacturing base, there has been no compensatory growth in service sector employment.
> (*The Anatomy of Job Loss: the How, Why and Where of Employment Decline*, Methuen, 1982, p. 6)

Such developments are highly significant for understanding the social organisation of work and the shape of the contemporary occupational structure in Britain.

The contemporary occupational structure in the UK

In 1960, 35.8 per cent of total employment in Britain was in manufacturing industry. By 1975 the proportion had dropped to 30.9 per cent, and by 1982 it was around 26 per cent. The trend has continued. Job losses in large manufacturing plants have become daily news items, a sign of industrial and economic decline in Britain. In 1983–84, for the first time in 150 years, Britain actually *imported* more manufactured goods than it exported. The term *deindustrialisation* has been invented to describe these transformations, another result of which is that as the percentage of people engaged in manufacturing employment – largely 'manual work' – has declined, 'service sector', 'non-manual' work has grown.

Decline is especially notable in industries which had been of greatest importance during the early years of industrialisation: textiles and clothing, metal manufacture and engineering. Growth in 'services' has largely been in insurance, banking and finance, education and health services, and 'miscellaneous services', such as catering and personal services. Since World War II the proportion of 'non-manual', 'white-collar' jobs has grown from just over 30 per cent in 1948 to a little under 50 per cent by the late 1970s. In the 1980s this growth has been halted as a result of the recession and public-sector employment cutbacks. Despite this, the stereotypical worker – 'blue collar', 'manual', working in a factory – is now in a minority. The UK is not alone in these trends; most of the advanced industrial societies have seen a decline in the relative importance of manual employment in manufacturing. As Nigel Harris recently wrote, 'By 1982, more than twice as many people sold McDonald's hamburgers in the United States as made steel; there were more people employed in retail and wholesale trade than in the whole of manufacturing' (*Of Bread and Guns: the World Economy in Crisis*, Penguin Books, 1983).

Such changes have been accompanied by the growth of the *casualisation* of the workforce – that is, as the number of full-time manufacturing jobs has been declining so has the number of *part-time* jobs been increasing. Between 1960 and 1980 in Britain part-time jobs doubled to 4.4 million, while the number of full-time jobs fell by 2 million. Most of the increase in part-time employment has been in the service sector, and 4 million of the part-timers are women. Part-time employment in 1984 accounted for 21 per cent of all employment, compared with 10 per cent in 1961.

Nor does employment in the expanding occupations necessarily ask for more 'skill' or offer better conditions of service than 'manual' work: service-sector work generally involves cleaning and caretaking. Hotels and catering, sport and recreation, the leisure and tourism industries employ mainly sales, clerical and unskilled staff. Many jobs are part-time, seasonal and low-paid. Additionally, as Ken Roberts has pointed out, 'Enabling individuals still working normal hours to enjoy normal leisure requires leisure professionals to sacrifice their own evenings, and weekends' ('Leisure', in M. Haralambos (ed.), *Developments in Sociology*, volume 2, Causeway Books, 1986).

Increasingly, the 'typical' British worker is no longer manual or male. The male labour force fell from 16.3 million in 1961 to less than 15.4 million in 1984, while the female labour force increased over the same period from 8.5 million to 10.8 million (*Employment Gazette*, May 1985). Women now represent 40 per cent of the labour force compared with less than 35 per cent in the early 1960s. The changes reflect both the increased participation of married women in the labour force (61 per cent were 'economically active' in 1984 according to the General Household Survey) and the move toward 'casualisation' on the part of employers. Such methods as subcontracting and employing people on temporary contracts, as well the growing use of part-timers, who are predominantly female, have been adopted as employers have sought more 'flexibility' – and lower wage costs.

Unemployment – the root of the crisis?

The most visible and, for millions, the most painful symptom of economic change in the advanced industrial societies has been the re-emergence of mass unemployment in the late 1970s and 1980s. Notwithstanding the debate about the measurement and definition of unemployment, registered unemployment in the twenty-four countries which make up the Organisation for Economic Co-operation and Development (OECD) and which include the USA, Canada, the UK, France, West Germany, Japan, Denmark and Sweden – that is, *the advanced industrial capitalist countries* – rose from a total of 8 million in the late 1960s to almost 15 million in 1975. The figure steadied until 1979, when it again grew rapidly. In 1983, 32 million people in OECD countries were registered as unemployed. Official figures do not tell the whole story either, as we shall see. They tend to *undercount* significantly the real number of people without paid employment who would like work if it was available, especially the young, women with young and old dependants, and, increasingly, men near to official retirement ages. Studies in different countries have confirmed that official figures should be substantially increased in order to give a more accurate picture of the true extent of unemployment.

The rate of unemployment in the UK has been well above the average for other advanced capitalist countries (see Table 2.1).

Table 2.1   Comparable international unemployment rates, January 1986 (per cent)

USA	Canada	Japan	France	Germany	Sweden	GB
6.7	9.8	2.7	10.2	7.8	2.6	13.2

Note: Figures are prepared on an 'approximately comparable' basis by the US Bureau of Labor Statistics each month.

Source: *Unemployment Bulletin*, No. 20, Summer 1986, published by the Unemployment Unit, 9 Poland Street, London.

Concentration on the annual average unemployment figures can distort the picture by ignoring group differences. The unequal burden of unemployment does have considerable social, economic and even political implications. For example, the latest survey of racial disadvantage in Britain carried out by the Policy Studies Institute confirmed patterns found in previous research: 'people of West Indian and Asian origin . . . are more likely than white people to be unemployed' (C. Brown, *Black and White Britain: the Third PSI Study*, Heinemann, 1984, p. 293). In a summary of official survey data *New Society* ('Black people and employment', 17 Oct. 1986, p. 44) revealed that in 1984 the rate of unemployment for black people in Britain was 20.4 per cent, compared with only 10.6 per cent among their white counterparts. Within the ethnic minority population further differences existed: the Bangladeshi and Pakistani community suffered the worst unemployment, a rate of 30.6 per cent, followed by those of West Indian origin, with 23 per cent. Further, whereas black women constitute only 3.7 per cent of the labour force, they account for 6.7 per cent of unemployed women

Perhaps the most frequently researched area, however, has been youth unemployment. In Table 2.2 it can be seen how youth unemployment rose between 1973 and 1982 in some of the major

Table 2.2   *Youth unemployment rates, 1973–1982 (percentages of youth labour forces)*[1]

	1973	1982
USA	9.9	17.0
Japan	2.3	4.4
France	4.0	20.3
West Germany	1.0	7.0[2]
Italy	12.6	27.4[2]
UK	3.3	19.8[2]

[1] age 16 to 24
[2] 1981 figures

Source: P. Armstrong *et al.*, *Capitalism since World War II*, Collins, 1984.

OECD countries. As we will see in Chapter 5, many authors have interpreted the resulting changes in the education and training of young people as a vindication of the view that the relations of production in work cast a very 'long shadow' over personal development in capitalist society.

Unemployment results from an imbalance between the number of jobs available and the number of people actually seeking paid work. Full employment, in an ideal world, would exist when everyone who wanted a paid job could have one. In Britain successive governments after World War II were committed to the idea (for men, at least), and throughout the 1950s and 1960s national unemployment was kept to an average of 2 per cent or about 400,000 people. The growth in unemployment therefore indicates a rising imbalance between the supply and the demand for labour. In the case of young people, demographic trends have been important in determining the numbers offering themselves on the labour market. However, this is not the whole story As we have seen, there have been major institutional changes occurring at a global level specific to a particular stage in the development of capitalism.

Explaining the changes

In order to understand the significance of these changes we need to consider theories of economic change. We shall consider four perspectives – Market liberal theory, Neo–Durkheimian theory, Marxism and Feminism – representatives in social science of conservative, reformist and radical political viewpoints respectively, and assess the contribution of each to understanding the situation in contemporary Britain.

Market liberal theory

During the economic boom after World War II a broad political consensus emerged in Britain. The two main political parties generally accepted the idea of a 'mixed economy' – that is, a capitalist economy with some state enterprise, like the nationalised industries in coal and steel. Governments in the 1950s, 1960s and for much of the 1970s accepted certain responsibilities for welfare provision, and adopted economic policies designed to maintain more or less full employment. By the mid-seventies, however, this consensus had come under severe strain because of the changes taking place in the world economy. Market liberal theory (MLT) is the basis for the 'radical right' attack on the post-war consensus, of which, in political terms, Mrs Thatcher in the UK and President Reagan in the USA are the two best examples.

MLT is less strictly a *sociological* theory than the other approaches. It stems from the ideas of free market economists such as **Adam Smith** and **John Stuart Mill**, and the twentieth-century figures **F. A. Hayek** and **Milton Friedman**. From the perspective of MLT the main problem facing the British economy is that there are too many 'imperfections' in the market for goods and services, including labour. Most of all there has been too much government intervention in the economy and too much power ceded to the trade unions. Both these developments are responsible for economic crisis. Government spending on services and public employment and trade-union strength in defending jobs and gaining improvements in conditions and wages has lead to *inflation*. Profit margins for employers have fallen dramatically, and many have gone into liquidation as a result, leading to increased *unemployment*. At the same time high rates of direct taxation by the government have taken away incentives to invest (for the top income bracket) and to work hard (for the poor).

MLT views trade unions as a particularly significant 'imperfection'. Workers have been able to secure improvements in wages, conditions and state services during the boom years, which have tipped the balance in their favour. For 'freedom' (that is, capitalism) to be restored the power of organised labour has to be confronted and reduced to its former size.

State intervention in the running of the economy, on the scale implied by the post-war consensus, is seen as highly restrictive of personal liberties, unnecessary, misguided and fundamentally disruptive of the capitalist free market system, which if left alone would produce full employment and rising living standards. State intervention *is* necessary so that individuals can pursue their own interests unmolested by others, especially trade unions, but beyond this minimal, 'policing' role it is felt to be unnecessary. MLT points toward a conservative solution to the crisis, favouring unfettered capitalism, lower taxes, restrictions on trade unions and the creation of a new entrepreneurial spirit via 'people's capitalism'.

MLT sees the relationship between employers and employees as essentially a harmonious one. Both workers and management share the same goals and ultimate interests of maximising output, profits and wages. It is a 'unitary' view of industrial relations, which tends to regard conflict as rather unnecessary, the result of misunderstanding or mischief – in short, pathological. In society at large this view may be the dominant one. Certainly it is the view most often fostered by a large number of employers, and found among workers as well. From another point of view the policies which stem from MLT – restrictive monetary policy, cutbacks in welfare, tax cuts (especially at the top, to encourage investment), privatisation and deregulation, and legislation to weaken trade unions – have merely served 'to restructure capital in favour of the giant companies and at the expense of labour' (M. Barratt Brown, *Models in Political Economy*, Penguin Books, 1984). Other sociological perspectives on work and the economy take this conflict of interest between employer and worker more or less for granted, though they very much differ over the meaning and significance of it, as we will see.

Neo-Durkheimian theory

For **Emile Durkheim**, writing in 1893, underpinning all societies lies a form of 'social solidarity', a moral order, that holds society together. The movement from *traditional* to *modern* society marks a shift in the type of social solidarity, from *mechanical* to *organic* solidarity. As modern society develops, an increasingly *complex division of labour* emerges and a process of *structural differentiation* of roles occurs. Work becomes specialised, people have their separate roles and skills. The central question for Durkheim was how social order and stability could be maintained in societies with an increasingly complex division of labour (*The Division of Labour in Society*, Macmillan, 1984 edition). Although often portrayed as a 'conservative', arguing that 'organic solidarity' based on the interdependence of those who have differentiated functions would and *should* develop, thus ignoring any division of interests between employers and sellers of labour, he did recognise three 'abnormal' forms: an 'anomic' division of labour in which inadequate normative regulation for solidarity in econ-omic life prevails; a 'forced' division of labour in which social inequalities do not match 'natural inequalities' (that is, there is no equality of opportunity); and inadequate co-ordination of productive activities within an enterprise, which can lead to employees being 'insufficiently occupied' and 'operations being carried on without any unity'.

Neo-Durkheimian theory stems from these ideas, arguing that the contemporary situation in the advanced industrial societies resembles Durkheim's 'abnormal forms'. Economic life rests upon a moral foundation which modern industrial societies tend to disrupt. Thus it is not possible to explain the problems of the British economy in terms of an *economic* theory alone. Notions such as 'free competition', 'consumer sovereignty' and even 'the market', are little more than ideas which are not found in their pure form in society. Economic theories tend to assume that the economy contains self-regulating tendencies. MLT, for example, suggests that the individual pursuit of self-interest will lead to the common good. Neo-Durkheimians, on the contrary, argue that the competitive market economy contains inherent tendencies toward social disorder and inequalities which are disruptive to the health of society.

In 'The current inflation: towards a sociological account' (in F. Hirsch and J. H. Goldthorpe (eds), *The Political Economy of Inflation*, Martin Robertson, 1978) **John Goldthorpe** argued that problems generated by the 'anomic' division of labour – wide-spread inequalities in wealth and income, restricted opportunities for personal advancement and mistrust in industrial relations – culminated in the late 1970s in a round of wage claims by strong trade unions seeking to maintain their differential rewards in the midst of increasing economic decline and rising unemployment. The result was to fuel inflation as unions tried to 'leap-frog' over the next group of workers' wage increase. In mature market societies, such as Britain, inequalities of opportunity in education and rewards from occupation are readily apparent to its members. This encourages comparisons across the range of the social order. The traditional status order has been disrupted, and in the absence of an accepted moral basis for inequality between the social classes, a secure moral community, a competitive struggle can also develop *within* classes.

For Goldthorpe, therefore, inflation in Britain in the 1970s was 'wage-led'. There was little community of interest within the working class and no body strong enough to bring capital and labour together to settle the differences. During the 1970s the state did try to act in a *corporatist* way, but it failed because it lacked moral cohesion and legitimation. Neo-Durkheimian theory views the free market ideal, of unrestrained capitalism, as having many undesirable consequences: increased inequality, conflict, unemployment and so on. Neo-Durkheimian theory points to a 'reformist' solution to economic problems, such as the policies proposed by the main political opposition, especially the Labour Party, whereby the state is given the leading role in regenerating the economy and creating the conditions for social stability. More generally, Goldthorpe's point is that an *adequate* explanation of economic problems must include a *sociological* explanation of the underlying social relations and processes. Abstract economic theory is too crude a model for understanding the real world. Let us now turn to a perspective which shares these concerns, but has significantly different concepts and conclusions: Marxism.

Marxist theory

Because many people's memories were dominated for years by the experience of the post-war economic boom, there was a tendency, until recently, to take continual economic growth for granted. There is still an inclination to think that the present recession is a deviation from a 'normal' pattern of expansion. For Marxists, however, the dynamic and *cyclical* nature of capitalist development is the starting point for understanding the contemporary decline of Britain (see Fig. 2.1).

Fig. 2.1 **Long booms and associated industries**
A cycle of booms and slumps can be traced from the early
days of industrialisation 200 years ago. Long booms that
have lasted for about twenty-five years have been followed
by long depressions of roughly the same duration. In the
1920s a Russian economist, N. D. Kondratieff, detailed
these cycles, called 'the Kondratieff Wave', showing how
each long boom has been closely associated with the growth
of one or more particular industry: textile manufacture;
railway building; electricity and shipbuilding; the motor car
and the aeroplane; and now, the computer and automation.

Dates	Industry	
1790–1815	Cotton	Mechanisation of spinning
1848–73	Textiles	Mechanisation of spinning and weaving
	Engineering	Production by machine of textile machinery, steam engines and locomotives
1896–1921	Engineering	Batch production; marine engineering; motor cars
	Steel	Bulk production
	Electrical engineering	
	Chemical engineering	Science-based industries
1945–74	Motor cars	
	Mechanical and electrical consumer durables	Assembly-line mass production
	Petro-chemicals	Continuous-flow process

Source: CSE Microelectronics Group, *Microelectronics: Capitalist Technology and the Working Class*. CSE Books, 1980, p. 4.

Marxist theory views capitalism as a system liable to self-generated crisis and chronic instability, constantly moving from boom to slump. New products, new areas for investment and new methods and technologies of production are periodically developed in order to arrest the problem of *declining profitability*. A surplus population of workers – those thought to be 'economically marginal', such as women, the aged and immigrants – have often been used to smooth out such fluctuations by being employed in booms and laid off in slump conditions.

Marx argued that economic liberalism (MLT) was an inadequate analysis of the capitalist economy as it concentrated on the market, rather than looking at the workings of the *capitalist labour process*. Liberal economists failed to recognise that rather than being the end-point of world historical development, capitalism was a *mode of production*, like others that had come before it, which would eventually be superseded. The writings of Adam Smith and others were flawed by their treatment of the capitalist market as an unalterable fact of life, rather than, as Marx saw it, a particular stage in the development of human kind. Additionally, their analyses lacked attention to the class structure which underpinned the economic system.

The society in which Marx lived exhibited great extremes of wealth and poverty and, whereas the majority of the population were propertyless (apart from the ability to labour for others in return for a wage), a minority possessed virtually all the land, tools and money. He argued that from the standpoint of the merchant the distribution was fair: those who possess money (capitalists) are rewarded for taking risks by receiving a greater sum of money than the sum they parted with at the outset. Propertyless individuals still have their capacity to labour, their 'labour services', which they can sell on the market to the highest bidder like any other commodity. But the buying and selling of 'labour power', like any other commodity, creates the basis for class society.

Capitalism was similar to previous modes of production in so far as it was based upon *class divisions*, but it differed in a number of important respects. Crucially its development facilitates the growth of a 'class-in-itself', the working class (or proletariat) which is composed of all those people who are compelled to sell their 'labour power' in return for wages, which *could* become an active force aware of its common interests. Marxists emphasise the central role of the production or *labour process* in creating class divisions and consciousness. The experience and nature of work is thus decisive in the generation of class consciousness. As a 'class-for-itself', the proletariat could transform the social relations of production and establish the first classless society based upon the 'socialisation of the means of production' and production for use, rather than profit: society organised to meet people's needs, not the dictates of a dominant class.

Marxist accounts of the decline of Britain

It is perhaps little wonder that in the last twenty years, as the post-war economic boom began to fade, Marx's ideas have become influential in the social sciences. The British economy has shared in the crisis confronting all capitalist economies since the early 1970s: the phenomenon referred to as 'stagflation' (stagnation or industrial decline, in conjunction with inflation). As a *world system* capitalism develops in uneven and unstable ways. The process of capital accumulation – the search for profitable returns on investment – constantly moves resources away from some economies and towards others. The decline of manufacturing employment in the West can be seen as the result of the development of prospects for higher returns on investment in the Third World. At the same time the introduction of new technologies will inhibit the re-employment of people laid off in the 'First World'.

The specific problems of Britain – the fact that it has sustained consistently higher rates of unemployment and inflation than other advanced industrial capitalist countries – have received two opposing explanations from Marxist authors. The economic historian **Eric J. Hobsbawm** argued in *Industry and Empire* (Penguin Books, 1969, pp. 172–94) that the beginning of Britain's decline was to be found as far back as the *1860s*. He draws attention to the division of the British capitalist class into *industrial* and *financial* sectors, with the latter being predominant. The post-war decline of the UK economy is then traced to the motives, orientations and responses of this dominant section of the capitalist class, which continued to put overseas expansion before domestic development. Others have put forward the argument that the 'capital–labour' struggle is most important in explaining post-war decline. **Andrew Glyn** and **Bob Sutcliffe** (*British Workers,*

Capitalism and the Profits Squeeze, Penguin Books, 1972) and Andrew Glyn and **John Harrison**. (*The British Economic Disaster*, Pluto Press, 1980) are the chief exponents of the idea that organised workers have brought about the contemporary crisis of profitability in Britain. The retreat of British capital investment abroad is a *result* of the economic decline of the UK (and the opportunity to make high profits) and not a *cause* of it as in Hobsbawm's thesis. Glyn and Harrison argue: 'if British capital did turn overseas, this was largely because it was difficult to produce competitively for export from the UK' (*The British Economic Disaster*, p. 42). It was not the result of the disdain for industry among the capitalist class that lead to investment abroad but the strength of the first fully organised working class.

The Marxist perspective is undoubtedly most impressive. Its claim to be able to link changes of a global, economic nature to those on the shop-floor and in the office is persuasive. It also suggests that what happens in any one national economy, or occupational structure, such as 'deindustrialisation' and the decline of the manual working class, needs to be understood, not as the demise of capitalism, but as a transformation to a new stage. As a political theory it suggests that a revolution is still necessary to remove capitalism, but that such an event, or chain of events, cannot be predicted outside of specific analyses of particular societies. In Britain the economic policies of 'Thatcherism' are seen as a major setback to working-class and socialist advance. The quotation from M. Barratt Brown earlier sums up the general view. The economic crisis has been exacerbated by the state as it restructures the economy and the labour market in the interests of multinational capital. But the Marxist perspective is not the only radical perspective on economic change, and feminist writers have begun to look critically at 'malestream' social science.

Feminist perspectives on the crisis

Marxist feminists argue that women are employed in certain jobs and sectors of the economy – in order to perform the work of reproducing and servicing the labour force – as a result of patriarchal notions inherited from pre-capitalist social relations. Women are occupationally segregated, receive low pay and are treated differently from male employees. Employers help sustain the 'sexual division of labour' by organising employment opportuni-

Fig. 2.2 **The increase in women's employment**
Since the origins of wage-labour, wives and mothers have contributed to the family income whenever work is available, domestic responsibilities permit and economic need dictates. The recorded increase in married women's work in Britain in the past twenty years is evidence that more and more families are dependent on two incomes. The increasing proportion of married women in the labour market in the past five years or so must be set in the context of increasing male unemployment. . . . The picture is a complex and difficult one to interpret, but there is no evidence that the increase in married women's waged work is in itself an indication either of improved status or of changing role.

What is changing, however, is work organisation and work methods. Much of the work that women once performed in their own or somebody else's home has been transformed . . . by the intervention of the market . . . today there are more office cleaners working for contract cleaning companies, and waitresses, maids and cleaners in hotels and restaurants, than there are domestic servants in private houses. Women are doing the work that they have always done, only now they are employed by a firm or company, their hours of work and methods of payment are to some extent regularised, their relationship to the state through taxation and national insurance more formalized. In these ways married women's waged work has become more visible. The rapid expansion of the service sector in most capitalist economies has been mainly responsible for the filling out of the statistics of women's economic activity rates in the Censuses since 1945. But what this marks is the extension of commodity production, not a change in women's role.

(S. Alexander, Introduction to M. Herzog, *From Hand to Mouth*, Penguin Books, 1980, pp. 19–20)

ties to meet 'women's needs'; hence part-time work and shifts are designed to enable married women with children to perform the two jobs of wage worker and unpaid housewife. The re-organising of the occupational structure, toward more female employment, especially part-time, in 'services', can thus be seen not really as the result of more and more women 'doing it for themselves', but to the changing possibilities which capital has seized for organising productive employment (see Fig. 2.2).

This also means that the Marxist view of women as part of the 'surplus population' of labour is problematic. The division of labour is 'gendered' (see I. Breugel, 'Women as a reserve army of labour' in *Feminist Review*, No. 3, 1979). Other feminists, although attracted to Marxism in some respects, argue that it is necessary to place the concepts of *gender* and *patriarchy* at the centre of analysis, rather than class. The study of work should therefore deal with *unpaid* as well as paid labour; work which does not easily fit into the 'manual'/'non-manual' division, such as the 'people work' of cooking, cleaning and caring, which is monopolised by women; and gender relations at work – that is, the way gender is used by employers to divide the workforce and by male workers to claim privileged positions and better pay. This perspective has little to say about the solution to the jobs crisis, but raises serious issues about the complexities involved in transforming the status quo in work.

Conclusions

This chapter has sought to provide an overview of some of the changes taking place in the economy and their impact on work. We have looked at four competing attempts to explain the crisis. There is little disagreement that there is a crisis, but the perspectives differ over which aspects of the crisis are the cause, which are the symptoms and what needs to be done about it. It should be immediately apparent that there is little way of evaluating these approaches except in terms of their *social consequences*. MLT and Neo-Durkheimian theory share a concern for moral regeneration, although for the former this would involve the creation of an 'enterprise culture' of small firms, wider share ownership and minimum state intervention, whereas for the latter this would only help to sustain the problem of moral 'anomie'. In many ways Neo-Durkheimian theory is an argument for a return to a 'corporatist' solution to economic decline – where the state allows trade unions and employers' associations to influence state decisions in return for those bodies controlling their members.

For the Marxist, as both these approaches support the continued existence of the capitalist system, the real source of the problems remains untouched by them. Whether a more 'free-market' solution or a more 'state-interventionist' solution is adopted, both approaches are framed within the assumption that the capitalist system is unalterable and inevitable. So long as it remains, however, British society must remain potentially unstable and conflictual. Of course the Marxist account of socialist revolution is also problematic, particularly in so far as it remains weak in understanding the importance of gender and ethnic relations in society. But because contemporary Western societies remain capitalist in their general basic character – production for profit remains the main dynamic impetus; ownership of private property, particularly capital, remains highly unequal; and conflict between classes still occurs – Marx's ideas and the Marxist perspective more generally retain 'a core of relevance to analysing those societies' (Anthony Giddens, *Sociology*, Macmillan, 1982, p. 71). In the study of work, employment and unemployment this is especially true, as well shall see in the rest of Part 2.

3 Theoretical traditions

Explaining and studying work

A distinctive feature of sociological study is the recognition that *theoretical concepts* are necessary in order to *explain* and *understand* any social phenomena. Theories both suggest what to look for and help interpret the findings of empirical social researech. This chapter will review the major theoretical traditions in the sociological study of work which existed until the late 1960s. First it is worth briefly considering theories and concepts which the 'classical' social scientists produced in the midst of the great social and economic changes of the eighteenth, nineteenth and early twentieth centuries.

The division of labour

Adam Smith (1723–90), the eighteenth-century classical economist, wrote, in 1776:

> The greatest improvement in the productive powers of labour and the greater part of skill, dexterity and judgement with which it is anywhere directed, or applied seem to have been the effects of the division of labour.
> (*The Wealth of Nations* (1776), Penguin Books, 1982, p. 109)

Smith, along with other 'classical economists', was greatly impressed by the newly emerging industrial division of labour. The predominant method of production before the Industrial Revolution, *handicraft*, was giving way to *machine production*; *home-based* production was giving way to the *factory*; and, because of *specialisation*, production could be carried out *concurrently* (that is, all aspects of the production process could be carried out simultaneously). For Smith, the changes in the organisation of production had three great advantages over old methods of production:

This great increase in the quantity of work, which, in conse-
quence of the division of labour, the same number of people
are capable of performing, is owing to three different circumstances; first, to the increase of dexterity in every particular
workman; secondly, to the saving of the time which is
commonly lost in passing from one species of work to another;
and lastly, to the invention of a great number of machines
which facilitate and abridge labour, and enable one man to do
the work of many.

(*Ibid.*, p. 112)

Smith gives a famous example of pin-making:

One man draws out the wire; another straights it; a third cuts
it; a fourth points it; a fifth grinds it at the top for receiving
the head: to make the head requires three distinct operations;
to put it on is a peculiar business, to whiten the pins is another;
it is even a trade by itself to put them into the paper; and the
important business of making a pin is, in this manner, divided
into about eighteen distinct operations.

(*Ibid.*, p. 110)

The social division of labour of pin-making was thus replaced in
factories by a *detail* or *technical division of labour* (see Reading 8.1).
What Smith did not point out was that this had the effect of
making workers dependent on capitalist employers. Under a
detail division of labour, workers know only a small part of the
process involved in producing a commodity. Additionally, as
Charles Babbage noted a half century after Smith, this gave the
capitalist an added advantage:

The master manufacture, by dividing the work to be executed
into different processes, each requiring different degrees of skill
or of force, can purchase exactly that precise quantity of both
which is necessary for each process; whereas, if the whole work
were executed by one workman, that person must possess
sufficient skill to perform the most difficult, and sufficient
strength to execute the most laborious, of the operations into
which the art is divided.

(Quoted in H. Braverman, *Labor and Monopoly Capital*,
Monthly Review Press, 1974, pp. 79–80)

In short, as Braverman says, 'in a society based upon the purchase and sale of labor power, dividing the craft cheapens its individual parts' (ibid.).

Smith is regarded as the founder of modern economics, for he outlined in the rest of *The Wealth of Nations* the ideals of free enterprise, the pursuit of self-interest and *laissez-faire* (that is, the principle of 'letting things be', of minimal government interference in the economy). Smith's ideas are an important ingredient of contemporary Market liberal theory. Many features of his writings were accepted by the major nineteenth-century critic of capitalism, **Karl Marx** (1818–83), but he emphasised quite different results of the division of labour.

Exploitation and allienation at work

The problem with the new capitalist system, for Marx, was that it constituted a form of systematic exploitation. The principal division at work was between the owners of factories and those who worked for them, that is, class divisions; the concentration of ownership and control of the means of production in the hands of the few provided the basis for the exploitation of the many; and the objective facts of exploitation were matched by the subjective experience of alienation.

The capitalist system was exploitative, not because of any duplicity or cheating on the part of the employers, but because of the way in which the *system* worked. Wealth was produced by the labour of workers, but a part of this wealth was taken from them by the owners of industry in the form of *profit*. People cannot find real satisfaction by working in a system which is based on their own exploitation. Hence workers are *alienated* from the product of their labour because of the property relations under capitalism. They do not own the product of their labour, but instead, in return for selling their *labour power* (*ability* to labour) they receive a wage which enables them to purchase the 'means of subsistence'. Anthony Giddens has written: 'What really distinguishes capitalism as a form of economic system is that labour (power) *itself* becomes a commodity, bought and sold on the market' (*The Class Structure of the Advanced Societies*, Hutchinson, 1981, p. 84). Unlike other commodities, however, the exchange of labour power cannot be instantaneous; the employer obtains the employee's *potential for work*, and to make use of this he has to control and direct the activities of the employee while under his employment. This loss of autonomy at work was, for Marx, another feature of alienation. Worse still, alienation meant not only lack of control over the job, its design or organisation but also lack of human contact with employers or workmates and separation from what Marx considered to be 'human nature', the ability to create and recreate the natural world through the act of labour. It applies to *everyone* in a capitalist society, not just workers in a factory or office. Capitalism is a kind of grand game in which individual capitalists compete with other capitalists for control over markets and with workers over the appropriation of *surplus value*.

Marx's critique of capitalism is a *holistic* one. The entire economic system generates impoverished work experiences and conditions of life in general. Attempts may be made to enrich and improve working conditions, and people are likely to seek to escape alienation in non-work, leisure activities, but the underlying, system-generated problems will remain.

The division of labour in society

For **Emile Durkheim** (1858–1917), the division of labour in society was a *moral* phenomenon: a positive, stabilising *social fact*, related to the way in which modern society was co-ordinated. Until it was properly developed and the upheaval involved in the emergence of modern industrial society died down, however, the problem of 'pathological forms' – most notably, 'anomie' – would mark many aspects of social life. Anomie – a social condition where norms and moral rules break down leaving people not knowing how to act – stems from weak social 'regulation'. In the study of work behaviour his ideas have been used especially in the study of industrial relations, which can be seen as an arena bound by rules of procedure and negotiation.

Durkheim's emphasis on *industrial* rather than *capitalist* society led him to view problems which existed in the workplace as temporary and 'abnormal', rather than systematically produced by the economy. The narrow focus of industrial sociologists on 'workplace behaviour' in the first few decades of the twentieth century has sometimes been seen as due to the influence of his writing.

Industrial sociology

In the first fifty years of the twentieth century the sub-discipline of industrial sociology was much influenced in its research by practical problems confronting industry. The focus of attention shifted away from that of the classical social scientists to narrower issues of labour relations, the behaviour and attitudes of *workers* and a general concern for the study of 'pathologies in the division of labour', aimed at improving company efficiency and so boosting company profits.

The writings of **Frederick Winslow Taylor** (1856–1915) on *scientific management*, and later, research conducted by **Elton Mayo** (1880–1949) and colleagues at Harvard University (the Human Relations tradition) are often taken as the starting points for reviews of the stages of development of industrial sociology. Put simply, Taylor firmly believed that money was the main incentive to work and that by linking productivity to pay he could ensure increased output. This view was then questioned, largely because, when strictly adhered to, it had created many problems in industrial relations. Theoretically, it treated workers as though they worked in isolation rather than in complex *informal social groups*. In the 1920s investigations by the human relations researchers into the culture and conditions of the work group and their impact on output (known as the *Hawthorne Experiments*, after the factory where they were conducted in Chicago) revealed the importance of *group norms* in establishing, for example, what was considered to be a fair day's work. These experiments showed that the key to understanding worker behaviour lay within *the group*, and the focus of attention turned from the isolated individual to the individual within the work group.

Typical of developments up to World War II industrial sociology was quite rightly accused of managerial bias by some post-war sociologists. In the 1970s Harry Braverman (see Chapter 4) argued that both scientific management and the human relations tradition were attempts to 'habituate the worker to the capitalist mode of production'. They were not the sciences of work so much as the sciences of management, value-laden through and through. It is debatable if Taylor should be included in a review of the study of sociology, but his ideas were based on the observation of the work process and thus provide a beginning to later developments. Mayo is a more complex character to assess and was undoubtedly influenced by an interpretation of Durkheim's writings. Both writers, however, lacked an adequate understanding of the wider social and economic context within which work takes place. (For a useful review of both authors, see M. Rose, *Industrial Behaviour: Theoretical Developments since Taylor*, Penguin Books, 1975.)

Technology, work satisfaction and alienation

In the 1950s and early 1960s, interest developed in the relationship between *technology* and worker attitudes and behaviour. **Robert Blauner**'s *Alienation and Freedom* (Chicago University Press, 1964) is a good example. 'Automation' was the buzz-word at the time, heralding a future where arduous labour would be replaced by machines operated by computers and as a result leisure would become more central to life than work. It was thought that the type of technology used in a factory had a crucial effect on the worker. It affects the amount of satisfaction to be had from the work because it determines the size and structure of the work group, as well as how the job is done. Craft industries, for example, are characterised by technology that permits workers a great deal of skill while working in small groups. At the other extreme, mass production is repetitive, low in skill and occurs in large, loose-knit groups. Job satisfaction, and therefore the amount of alienation experienced by workers, varies according to the technology used.

Blauner's study is an interesting example of how theoretical concepts need to be carefully handled. Although he restored technology, the division of labour and alienation as central to industrial sociology, he also sought to distinguish his research from Marxism. Blauner asserted that there were four 'dimensions of alienation', which he contrasted with four non-alienative states:

Alienation	Non-alienative states
Powerlessness	Control
Meaninglessness	Purpose
Isolation	Social integration
Self-estrangement	Self-involvement

Although the lists may be seen as a useful way of summarising the *psychology* of alienation, they clearly indicate a departure from the social, *structural* conception of alienation, as used by Marx. Blauner argued that alienation was related to types of work, levels of skill and technology (see Fig. 3.1). Over time, levels of alienation at work took on the shape of an 'inverted U-curve'.

Automated production techniques (where mechanical or electronic devices, such as computers, automatically operate a production process and thus replace human operatives) actually have the effect of returning to the worker 'a sense of control over his technological environment, that is usually absent in mass production factories' (*Alienation and Freedom*, p. viii). Although the worker may not always be fully integrated into the firm or totally satisfied, the trend is toward more worker involvement and thus a more contented workforce overall. Blauner can be seen as an advocate of the 'upgrading thesis', an idea that was widely held in the 1950s and the early 1960s. Although there was going to be less work about in the future, especially of the 'manual' kind, what work existed was going to demand greater skills and creativity than in the past. A more highly educated workforce would be necessary. Coupled with the decline of arduous work and the decline of the manufacturing 'working class', profound changes in the very fabric of society were underway, towards a more middle-class, post-industrial society. The effects on the rest of society were compounded by two other trends: firstly, an apparent decline in work-based conflicts; and, secondly, a belief that workers were becoming more interested in leisure activities and consumption as central life interests, and were thus taking a much more 'instrumental' attitude to work. Despite differences of opinion, the general view among sociologists in the 1950s and 1960s was that work, and especially alienation from work, were of declining importance in the modern world.

By the end of the 1960s, however, considerable business and governmental concern was being expressed in most of the advanced industrial societies about the revolt *against* work. High

Fig. 3.1 **Blauner on technology and alienation**

Type of work →	Craft	Machine minding ↓	Assembly line ↓	Automated process ↓
Type of production/ product →	No standarised product	Mechanisation and standardisation	Rationalisation Standardised product	Rationalistion Uniform product
Level of skill →	High	Low	Low	Responsibility and understanding needed
Level of allienation →	Low	High	Highest	Low

Source: M. O'Donnell, *A New Introduction to Sociology*, London, Nelson 1981, p. 366.

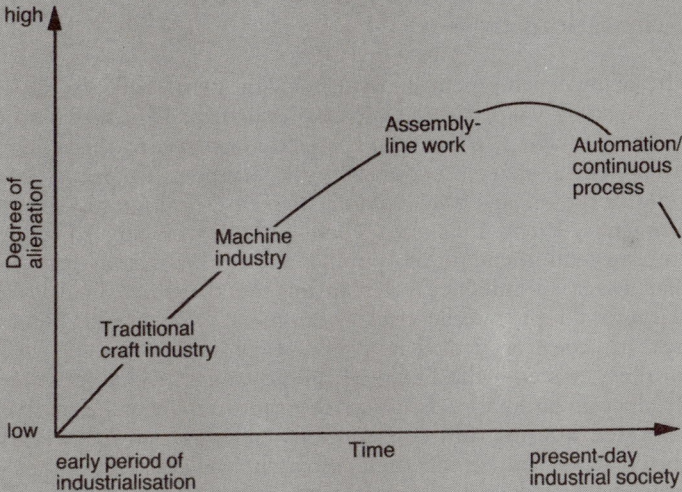

Source: T. Bilton *et al.*, *Introductory Sociology*, London, Macmillan, 1981, p. 646.

rates of absenteeism, labour turnover, low productivity, the apparent rejection of the traditional work ethic, and various types of industrial disruption, all added up to a crisis which industrial sociology had not foreseen. Why was there such a mismatch?

Paul Thompson suggests that part of the problem with studies such as Blauner's was that they took the nature and design of technology at work for granted as a *neutral form*, a technical matter, rather than seeing it as designed to secure control over the workforce and thus increase *surplus value* (in *The Nature of Work*, Macmillan, 1983, p. 19). Additionally, as a result of the methodology adopted (largely questionnaire-based), Blauner failed to study actual workplace *relationships* and the work *process* itself. Because the focus of attention was on *workers* rather than *work*, the majority of studies failed to get an accurate or objective picture of the importance and nature of work in modern society.

Orientations to work

The main development in British sociology of work in the 1960s was a study carried out by **J. Goldthorpe, D. Lockwood, F. Bechoffer** and **J. Platt** into the factors *external* to the work situation which shaped people's work attitudes or *orientations* (J. Goldthorpe *et al.*, *The Affluent Worker*, 3 volumes, Cambridge University Press, 1968–69). These authors were able to refute the embourgeoisement thesis, popular in the 1950s and early 1960s, that increased affluence was causing the British manual working class to adopt middle-class (bourgeois) values and life-styles. Instead, they argued that a new type of 'privatised', affluent worker existed who worked in advanced technology, mass-production industries (such as the motor industry) and lived in relocated housing and communities (such as Luton, in Bedfordshire, where much of their research was carried out). These privatised workers had orientations to work outside the supposedly traditional proletarian ones, focused on the local community and comradeship at work. Instead, privatisation was the effect of living in a consumer society where private, family needs come to take priority over collectivistic ones. The result, in terms of work orientation, was a purely instrumental attitude, linked toward the pay packet, regardless of job satisfaction or other rewards intrinsic to the job done. Studies like this, taking into account factors such as family, friends and educational background, as well as work experience, were an improvement on previous attempts to explain worker behaviour. An individual's attitude to work will not only strongly affect his or her choice of job but also his experience and reaction to it. As Thompson suggests, however, work experience was 'read off' from survey responses, rather than through an examination of the actual organisation of work:

> the survey questions themselves often show[ed] little under-standing of the social relations embedded in the labour process . . . it is hardly surprising that most workers will reject statements saying that team work is impossible because employers and workers are really on the opposite side. Given that cooperation and antagonism between capital and labour necessarily exist side by side in work, such statements are transparently untrue
> (Paul Thompson, *The Nature of Work*, Macmillan, 1983, p. 32)

In order to explain worker unrest adequately it was felt necessary to get inside the places where the trouble lay.

Back to Work

Studies of daily life on the shop floor such as **Huw Beynon's** *Working for Ford* (Penguin Books, 1984, originally published in 1973), involved the author in intensive participant observation over five years at the Halewood factory in Liverpool. Beynon was able to reveal the persistence of *informal work groups* among the mass production assembly line, as well as many, less obvious, acts of worker *resistance* to managerial authority. Around the time that *Working for Ford* was published, other accounts of factory life were appearing in Europe and the USA. All of them became the centre of controversy. They recorded the factory conditions and subjective experience of workers, their reactions and attitudes, and revealed many of the social and political arrangements that had been taken for granted were under threat.

Social research had touched upon a raw nerve. Many more case studies and ethnographies of workplace relations have appeared since. Some have even set out to challenge the stereotypical view of 'work' as manual and, occurring only in a factory, the 'worker' as white and male. Research in the last ten years has reflected the new interest in the social relations of production and has considered work organisation, the nature of the employment relationship and issues of conflict and control at work. One author in particular can be seen as responsible for pushing the sociology of work in this direction: Harry Braverman. We shall look at his work in the next chapter.

4 Labour process theory and the nature of work

Introduction

Since the mid-1970s industrial sociology has undergone a dramatic transformation. Labour process theory (LPT), derived from the writings of Karl Marx in the nineteenth century, but given fresh impetus by **Harry Braverman**'s *Labor and Monopoly Capital: the Degradation of Work in the Twentieth Century* (Monthly Review Press, 1974), is responsible for much of the change. Braverman's book had an immediate and international appeal largely because it 'smashed through the academic barriers and offered the potential for a new intergrated approach to the study and history of work' (Craig Littler in *The Development of the Labour Process in Capitalist Societies*, Heinemann, 1982). It enabled researchers to see links between subjects previously treated in isolation – in subdisciplines such as industrial sociology, organisational analysis and industrial relations.

LPT focuses attention on the labour process – any organised system of activity whereby the human capacity to produce, results in a useful article or service – and thus on the nature and experience of work under particular economic and social conditions. In Parts 3 and 4 of *Capital*, volume 1, Marx outlined the development of capitalist manufacture from simple handicraft production to 'machinofacture': the use of machines in manufacturing. Braverman attempted to bring the analysis up to date. Contrary to most social science theory, he argues that the development in the twentieth century of large-scale industrial organisations under *monopoly capitalism* has led to an increased *degradation* of work. What Marx referred to as the *real subordination of labour* was only completed in the twentieth century.

The main symptoms of this are the loss of skills, creativity and control by the worker over his or her labour, and the increasingly sophisticated science and technology that management has at its disposal to hasten the *deskilling* process. Former possibilities for personal initiative, direction and control of the work process have

Fig. 4.1 **Technology and the production of biscuits**
At the beginning of the century, relatively little technology
was employed in biscuit factories. Huge sacks of flour, sugar
and other ingredients were manually lifted and emptied into
big vats where they were mixed in the right proportions and
to the right consistency by master bakers; the dough was
rolled by hand, cut to the requisite patterns, placed on
baking trays and put in large ovens. The baking process was
carefully checked and supervised by skilled workers and,
when done, the biscuits were laid off onto trays ready for
women workers to package and box. . . . By the 1930s,
lifting aids were being used, mixing machines were introduced, electric ovens had replaced other methods and
conveyor belts moved biscuits and dough around the
factory. Some manual heavy lifting had been mechanised,
most skills were intact. . . . By the 1960s dramatic changes
were in evidence. Virtually all the conventional skills had
been eliminated: the consistency of the mixtures was
monitored by electrical equipment and the results displayed
in a central control room, a standardised product was
ensured by a constant time of travel through ovens and
cutting was performed by machine. The only part of the
process which remained labour-intensive was the packaging
and the boxing. . . . Two reasons have been advanced by
biscuit factory manufacturers for this non-automated area.
First, that the packaging of biscuits is an extremely intricate
affair and any machinery designed to do it would be so
inflexible as to take six months to change any particular
packaging configuration. Second, that women, through
their 'natural' digital dexterity, are best suited to this repetitive, boring job.
(D. Albury and J. Schwartz, *Partial Progress: the Politics of
Science and Technology*, Pluto Press, 1982, pp. 44–5)

been gradually wrested from the workers and have become a part
of the machines they operate and the responsibility of managers
and supervisors. Fig. 4.1 illustrates these developments with
reference to biscuit manufacture, and in the next section we shall
discuss the component parts of the argument.

The deskilling thesis

Although he never uses the term (preferring 'degrading'), Braverman is generally regarded as putting forward a 'deskilling thesis' in his book. As Albury and Schwartz point out, their example highlights both 'the deskilling tendencies of capitalist technology and the way that such technology also reflects and reinforces the sexual division of labour'. As a Marxist, Braverman emphasises the need to take the nature and purpose of production under capitalism into account when analysing the conditions of work. He sees the design of jobs, the division of labour at work and its organisation as underpinned by the motive of accumulating capital through the extraction of *surplus value*. It is the logic of capital accumulation, not technological innovation, that dictates the organisation of work. The labour process can therefore only be understood fully by realising its *capitalist* origins. It reflects the fundamental antagonism between capitalists and workers. This conflict, and particularly the employer's need to maximise profits, dictates that the scope for worker's control of, and discretion at, work must be severely limited. The division of labour and the hierarchical nature of modern work organisations are not therefore simply in the interests of pure productivity and efficiency, as was asserted by theorists such as Adam Smith. The *technical (or detail) division of labour*, which developed in the nineteenth century, involves the division and further subdivision of tasks within a production process as a means to *control* the workforce. Furthermore, the technical division of labour, by breaking a job into its component parts, with different individuals specialising in different parts of it, also enables employers to hire less skilled, and thus cheaper, labour (known as the 'Babbage principle' after Charles Babbage).

Unlike Marx, who appeared to argue in the *Communist Manifesto* and elsewhere that capitalists secured control over their workforce in the nineteenth century when they simply introduced machinery which dictated the pace of work and made workers little more than appendages, Braverman argues that the *real subordination of labour* did not occur until the twentieth century. According to him it was not until the latter part of the nineteenth and beginning of the twentieth century that capitalists became fully aware of the importance of controlling their workforce through the design of jobs and organisation of work – in short, the division of labour at work. The introduction of new technology enabled managements to establish new working practices and relations. But ideas about managerial responsibility for the systematic analysis, and hence control, of the work process, only arose with the writings of industrialist **F. W. Taylor** (*The Principles of Scientific Management*, 1911, Harper & Row, 1947 edition). Taylor was the first theorist to acknowledge the importance for management to take up the systematic study and control of the planning of work. The essence of *scientific management* was the separation of planning how to do a job, in what time it should be done, and so on from actually doing it. *Execution* becomes separated from *conception*, and a special body of employees are entrusted with the planning and design of work tasks, while the bulk of the employees are restricted to simple, mundane tasks. 'Brain work', involving a certain amount of freedom and discretion, is removed from the shop floor and becomes the monopoly of a section of management. For Braverman, 'Taylorism' is *the* principle underpinning the entire modern capitalist mode of production.

Thus, according to Braverman, the hallmark of the nature of work under capitalist relations of production is a tendency toward 'deskilling'. The labour process under capitalism is constantly subject to it, and, as the twentieth century has progressed, more and more occupations – even those that were once seen as of high status, such as much 'white-collar' work – have been deskilled. From a worker's point of view possession of skilled status provides him or her with some power to resist managerial domination at work, and also improves his market situation, in terms of rewards and conditions. Braverman therefore rejects the idea that changes in the occupational structure in the twentieth century, especially in the post-World War II period – leading to more middle class, non-manual occupations – are a significant alteration in the contours of capitalist society. His view contrasts sharply with those who have argued that in the twentieth century work has increasingly been 'upskilled'. Instead, he suggests trends toward *proletarianisation* and *homogenisation*, in which more and more occupations have become marked by conditions similar to manual, factory, 'proletarian' work. Rather than permitting initiative, interest and autonomy, clerical work and jobs in the expanding service sector have been equally subject to the process of deskilling. Braverman thus challenges common distinctions made between skilled and unskilled, manual and non-manual, blue- and white-collar, and factory and office work. For him the terms 'worker' and 'working class' refer to everyone who has to work for a living: professionals and middle-class people, as well as those in routine white-collar and manual jobs.

The deskilling debate

Although Braverman's book was principally about the organisation of work in the USA, the framework of analysis he used was seen as broadly applicable to countries which developed in similar ways after industrialisation, such as the UK. But in the years since his death, in 1975, reviews, further elaborations and critical assessments have proliferated. The following are the main areas of debate.

Class consciousness and struggle

For a Marxist account, Braverman's book is relatively silent on the questions of class consciousness and class struggle. He admitted that his aim was merely to deal with the 'objective' content of class as shaped by the 'capital accumulation process', to deal with 'the working class as a class-in-itself, not as a class-for-itself' (Braverman, *Labor and Monopoly Capital*, 1974, p. 27). For some critics this has made it seem as if employers and managers have complete control over the labour process, with the role of conflict and struggle between capital and labour in shaping conditions at work down-played. The development of organisations such as trade unions to defend working-class interests is thus largely ignored by Braverman. Recently, studies of industrial relations and conflict have merged in critical dialogue with Braverman's ideas. Some of this research is discussed later.

Management and control

Critics have suggested that although Braverman was correct to view the growth of systematic management as a hallmark of the twentieth century, he was wrong about the pervasiveness of 'Taylorism'. **R. Edwards** (*Contested Terrain: the Transformation of the Workplace in the Twentieth Century*, Heinemann, 1979) depicts a series of *stages of control* arising out of the development of capitalist production and worker resistance. *Simple* or *personal* control exercised by employers in the nineteenth century gave way to more complex forms with the shift from competitive to monopoly capitalism. *Technical* control was introduced via assembly-line production as the pace and direction of the labour process could be directed by managerial staff. The danger with this 'strategy' is that it can lead to a common experience of work and thus the basis for worker opposition. *Bureaucratic* control enables management to divide the workforce, while at the same time tying it to the rules and regulations of the company. Companies using this form of control develop a hierarchical structure of jobs and rewards, access to which is governed by *internal labour markets* which *shelter* workers from market competition as reward for their loyalty. Edwards shows how each of these types of control still exists in US companies today, with the largest corporations favouring the more complex, bureaucratic model. By segmenting labour markets, employers divide and rule workforces which have become potentially unified by mass production.

Another example of the variable nature of managerial strategy is supplied in **Andy Friedmann's** *Industry and Labour* (Macmillan, 1977). He argues that managerial strategies for control of the workforce can range from *Direct Control*, where almost every piece of worker activity is tightly controlled and pre-determined by a managerial directive, to *Responsible Autonomy* where groups of workers are given freedom, within limits, to control their own methods of production and pace of work. Friedmann suggests that the method of control used depends in part on the importance and skills of the workers involved. Skilled workers in a central position in a company are allowed some job discretion, whereas unskilled workers who are poorly organised are more likely to be subject to direct control.

Although these arguments can be seen as an improvement on Braverman's, they have also been criticised recently, most notably for the assumption that there is *one* single successful managerial strategy. Instead, recent research has focused on the way in which management decisions about work organisation are often influenced by factors other than a shop-floor battle over the frontier of control – in particular, the *product market* circumstances of different companies and sectors, and the state of the economy in general.

Historical evidence

Historians with an interest in the development of industry in the USA and the UK have pointed out several flaws in Braverman's account. Apart from the view that he got the timing, extent and pace of deskilling wrong, a major criticism has been his idealised picture of the craft worker. The central place given to craft work obscures the fact that in the past a much larger proportion of the male workforce was engaged in activities such as mining and transport. Since there has not yet been much research, it is hard to know the actual range of mental activities and control that characterised their work. Indeed, Ray Pahl sees Braverman as one of those writers who postulates a 'golden age' of work, which follows on from a romantic tradition: 'as with similar myths referring to past times, the precise period that is held up for approval is always some time before a given author is writing.' (*Divisions of Labour*, Blackwell, 1984, p. 2) Employers might become dependent on the skills of their workers under certain conditions. Workers might be able to develop mechanisms of *social exclusion*, such as the *closed shop* to protect themselves against other workers. Labour market conditions, such as scarcity of labour, could also be used by the workforce against their employers. In short, Braverman may be responsible for over-rating the freedom and satisfaction arising from traditional working practices, and underplaying the ability of workers to resist employer strategies. These are issues for future research.

Feminist criticism

LPT emerged during the same period as the renewal of feminism, and Braverman's book was applauded for recognising that 'the working class has two sexes' – that is, the prominence he gave to the changing gender composition of the working class – as clerical, retail and service-sector work had expanded. However, feminists also pointed out that Braverman held a traditional view of work, a highly *productionist* account, which ignored the sexual division of labour and the ideologies about male and female roles, which determine the supply of female labour to capital. He tended to view women as part of the *industrial reserve army of labour*, a reserve that could be drawn upon by employers when there was a shortage (such as during the two World Wars), and also as a

source of cheap and unskilled labour. Such a view has some truth
to it, but it oversimplifies matters greatly. His analysis can be
faulted therefore for not being applicable to all forms of women's
employment. Some women are professionals, perform skilled
work (that is, work which involves complex competences, even
if it is not classified officially as skilled) and have undergone
reskilling (that is, they have gained new skills as old ones have
been destroyed). Additionally, in 1979 the economist **Irene
Bruegel** assessed the theory that women were a reserve army of
labour (in 'Women as a reserve army of labour', *Feminist Review*,
No. 3, pp. 12–23). She found that the situation was not merely
that women workers were more 'disposable' than men. Because
women earn lower wages than men and because they are concentrated in particular sectors of the occupational structure (see Table
7.2,   p. 78),   there   was   a   cushioning   effect   on   women's
unemployment in the period 1974–78. Women may be used to
undercut the higher wages demanded by male workers, and
because of occupational *segregation* they are much less disposable
than the reserve army thesis would suggest. Bruegel found that
women were more likely to be used as a reserve army of labour
in manufacturing, but not in the service sector, which is a major
site of women's employment. Another more recent issue has been
the point that Braverman assumed that deskilling was due to
management and not the actions of male trade unionists. Research
has revealed the extent to which sexist ideological assumptions
have influenced the organisation and nature of work (see Reading
8.4, pp. 97–9). Thus key groups of workers (for example,
skilled, organised male workers), as well as management can be
seen as having the power to shape the division of labour. Perhaps
the main point of the feminist critique is that Braverman did not
consider the sexual division of labour more widely, and in
particular the relationships between paid work and work outside
employment, such as unpaid domestic labour. Like most research
in the sociology of work he largely took male factory workers
as the norm against which other workers and forms of work
could be compared and assessed.

Despite the various weaknesses of the original, Braverman's
book has had an enormous impact on the sociological study of
work. For the last fifteen years the deskilling thesis has acted as
the *problematic* framing research. In the next section we will look
at some aspects of this research.

Post-Braverman research

Research since Braverman's death in 1975 has taken place in a context of worldwide economic recession, the rise of new technologies, and different responses by governments to the problems that these developments have brought with them. LPT has appeared very relevant in attempting to answer questions posed in this changing economic, political and social climate.

The nature of skill

Braverman criticised proponents of the *upgrading thesis* that work in modern, post-industrial society had become more skilled, demanding more know-how and training, arguing that social definitions and ideological notions enter into the definition of certain kinds of work as skilled. Thus Braverman raised questions about the conventional view of skill in industrial sociology (see Fig. 4.2). However, he has been criticised by feminists for failing to realise the full significance of a *social constructionist* view of skill

Fig. 4.2 **The notion of 'skill'**
Conventionally 'skill' is believed to involve some kind of learnt expertise in a variety of actions or procedures plus the mental ability to apply them effectively and resourcefully. In other words, it is thought that skill is an *objective* feature of a particular set of attributes or competences – because of the *knowledge* required to do them, or the *length of time* required to gain acceptance (or gain a qualification) as a 'skilled' person. Additionally a job is often called 'skilled' where it entails a significant amount of *autonomy* from control by an immediate superior. For example this is a key feature of occupations labelled *professions*. Industrial sociologists have become interested in the way in which groups of workers who wish to obtain greater security of tenure over their jobs, control over their work, or simply more pay than less 'skilled' co-workers, often use arguments about their *skilled* status as a justification for differential treatment.

for his own argument. Referring to the official classification of workers as skilled in the US Census, he showed how jobs had been reclassified over a period of time. The result was that most of the apparent differences between skilled, semi-skilled, unskilled, and even some occupations labelled 'professional', were largely illusory. As he states:

It is only in the world of census statistics, and not in terms of direct assessment, that an assembly line worker is presumed to have greater skill than a fisherman or oysterman, the forklift operator greater skill than the gardener or groundskeeper, the machine feeder greater skill than the longshoreman, the parking lot attendant greater skill than the lumberman or raftsman.

(Braverman, *Labor and Monopoly Capital*, p. 430).

He argued that many of the existing classifications of jobs gave the false impression that there was much more skill around in jobs in the contemporary labour market than there really was. When jobs labelled 'semi-skilled' were considered, it was obvious that most of them took only a few weeks, some only a few days or hours, to learn. There was little real skill involved in them at all. The same was true of British industry where the main distinguishing feature between the skilled and the semi-skilled, according to Braverman, quoting industrial sociologist Joan Woodward, is 'a matter of "years" of training, while the creation of "semi-skill" as against "no skill" is accomplished in "two to twelve weeks"' (*Labor and Monopoly Capital*, p. 432). Braverman's point, that the notion of 'skill' is heavily dependent on social definitions, conventions and labels, as much as on any attribute of the activity carried out itself, was well taken.

Following Braverman, researchers have gone in one of two directions. Some have explored the idea that skill labels are a *tool of management*, used to divide and rule their workforces, and thus enhance control. By *segmenting* the workforce, management can play one section off against others: skilled against semi-skilled, semi-skilled against unskilled, and so on. This is the situation revealed in a recent study by **Ruth Cavendish** (*Women on the Line*, Routledge & Kegan Paul, 1982). In the electrical components factory where she conducted her participant observation research she discovered the existence of *internal labour markets*, in which a variety of statuses and rewards within the firm were created and sustained by management. This was done not so much in the interest of company efficiency, to secure the most appropriately skilled workers to specific parts of the production process, as to reinforce social divisions along the lines of status, gender and race, and thus inhibit the possibility of unified worker resistance to managerial dictates.

Others, particularly feminists such as Ann Phillips and Barbara Taylor (in 'Sex and skill: notes towards a feminist economics', *Feminist Review*, No. 6, 1980, pp. 79–88) have been interested in the way skill labels have arisen as a product of *worker initiatives* to combat market pressure and deskilling. From this view skill is an 'ideological category imposed on certain types of work by virtue of the sex and power of the workers who perform it'. Well-organised groups of male workers have been able to resist managerial decisions over regrading that would affect their position and rewards. (Until recently a good illustration of this would have been male workers in the Ford Motor Company and the printworkers in Fleet Street; see H. Beynon, *Working for Ford*, Penguin Books, 1973, pp. 170–80, and Reading 8.3, pp. 96–7). Many women workers also use skills which are not defined as such – typing, preparing and serving food, mending and sewing clothes – often because they are learnt informally, at home, rather than over some recognised period of formal training. Additionally, trade unions can themselves be seen as responsible for not fighting to get women's jobs defined as skilled.

Critics of the 'social construction of skill' argument point to the fact that skill is more real and has more substance than is implied by Braverman. In particular, **David Lee** has shown in the case of craft work in Britain that its disappearance does not necessarily mean that all skill has been taken out of the work that replaces it on the shop floor. Some jobs, given or denied due recognition by employers and/or census classifiers, are skilled because of their *technical skill content* ('Beyond deskilling: skill, craft and class' in S. Wood, *The Degradation of Work?*, Hutchinson, 1982). Also, as Cynthia Cockburn indicates in Reading 8.3 (pp. 96–7), it is important to distinguish the different meanings of skill: as *objectively* defined complex competences; as *control* over conception and execution; and as *socially defined* and *subjectively* conceived occupational statuses, which may, or may not, be largely independent of the level of objectively defined competence. Perhaps there needs to be room, as Craig Littler suggests, for a *'weak' social* *construction theory of skill*, which recognises that all skilled jobs have *some* objective skill content, but it is the *collective organisation* of workers involved plus their *strategic position* within the production process, which gains a particular set of tasks a *skilled* label. Management may use skill labels, but so too do workers, in the context of the capitalist employment relationship.

New technology

Braverman marked a move away from the optimism as regards technology of the 1950s and early 1960s, and rebutted theories which verged on the deterministic, whereby the latest technologies were heralded as a means of enhancing working conditions and the quality of life in general. Braverman made the useful point that technology only gets adopted under specific *social and economic conditions*; there is no autonomous development of technology and science, abstracted from society. The course of human history is not merely a simple reflection of the evolution of science and technology. Instead, he placed the responsibility for the organisation of work in the realm of the *social relations of production*, into which the *forces of production* – new technology and science – are introduced.

Braverman's ideas were timely considering the arrival of new technology – the microchip and robotics – in the 1970s. There can be little doubt that new technology *can* deskill and degrade the experience of work. The negative aspects of the microchip have been widely reported (see, for example, CSE Microelectronics Group (*Microelectronics: Capitalist Technology and the Working Class*, CSE Books, 1980).

Recent research by **Rosemary Crompton** and **Gareth Jones** into clerical and administrative white-collar workers in local government, banking and life assurance has confirmed that deskilling has affected these areas also (*White-Collar Proletariat*, Macmillan, 1984). However, they suggest that the impact is not felt uniformly by the workforce, but is dependent upon such factors as position in the labour market and gender (see Fig. 4.3). In short, different starting places in the hierarchy of jobs leads to different experiences of deskilling.

Despite these arguments over of the deskilling thesis, some researchers have warned about the danger of viewing the intro-

Fig. 4.3 **Deskilling and gender in clerical work**
Braverman placed a question mark over the significance of
the post-war growth of white-collar, middle-class, occupations for altering the basic shape of the *class structure*. In
British sociology this view has been opposed by the research
of John Goldthorpe and his colleagues at Oxford University.
On the basis of the Nuffield Mobility Study (*Social Mobility
and Class Structure in Modern Britain*, 1980) they argue that
the expansion of white-collar employment in Britain since
World War II has permitted significant levels of *upward social
mobility* to administrative posts. In particular, this has
produced a new occupational grouping – *the service class* –
made up of professional, administrative and managerial
employees. Crompton and Jones linked this debate to the
issues of deskilling and gender relations at work in their
research. They found that deskilling had occurred, especially
as a result of automation and the reorganisation of office
work. Most routine clerical jobs were semi-skilled or even
unskilled – they took very little time to pick up. Official
classifications of jobs appear out of touch with the reality
of the work actually performed (for example, routine white-
collar work is equated with skilled manual work by the
Registrar General). Thus some support is given to Braverman. However, they are more cautious in their overall
conclusions because they found considerable differentiation
among the deskilled white-collar workers, rather than any
shift to a cohesive 'proletarian mass'. In particular, they
noted the difference between the position of women – 70 per
cent of the clerks – for whom promotion prospects were
very limited, and of men, for whom promotion was
expected and a real possibility. In short, they suggest that
Braverman's thesis may be appropriate for explaining
women's position in 'white-collar' employment, whereas
Goldthorpe's thesis may apply to men in office work.

duction of new technology as inevitably leading to deskillin
Such a view would ignore the fact that some new jobs and skills
are being created in turn. Just as the possibility of deskilling was
largely ignored by those theorists (such as Blauner) who in the

1950s and 1960s viewed automation and new technology as potentially liberating and less alienating, the issues of *reskilling* and even *upskilling* have, until recently, been left on the sidelines in the glow of Braverman's critique. Researchers are becoming increasingly sensitive to this possibility, however, and the implication that a *polarisation* of skills may be occurring, where alongside deskilling some workers either retain skills, learn new ones or take on those lost by workers lower down the jobs hierarchy. The introduction of new technology into the secretarial and clerical fields is a good example of this. Whether the development of these new skills compensate for the loss of the old is a debatable point. Only further research into the introduction of new technology in specific industries will provide us with the answer.

Conflict and co-operation at work

Since Braverman's book was published a shift in perspective has occurred in the way in which the employment relationship is conceived. It is increasingly recognised that it is in many ways a *contradictory* relationship. Increasingly, due in no small way to the emphasis which Braverman's thesis put on studying the work experience in detail, the relationship between employer and employee has been seen to involve elements of both conflict *and* co-operation. Capitalists must seek the co-operation of workers (even though they have the ultimate power to hire and fire, close down factories and relocate production), while workers must also seek to maintain the success of their enterprise – the particular industry, factory or office that employs them. To capture this 'essential tension' – 'between the need to regulate and dominate the production process versus the need to maximise the creativity and reliability of labour' (C. Littler and G. Salaman, *Class at Work*, Batsford, 1984, p. 90) – it has been suggested that there can be no *universal* statements made about conflict at work under capitalism. There are variations in the behaviour of capitalist firms. Managements do not all respond in the same way to similar economic situations. There is usually more than one solution for most problems. And since there is a degree of 'strategic choice' for management, the same is also likely to be true for the workforce. The general state of industrial conflict and power relations between management and workers in the current recession provides a number of illustrations of this.

It is widely believed that the fear of unemployment, together with new industrial relations laws, are influencing industrial relations behaviour. 'We've got three million on the dole, and another 23 million scared to death' (Ron Todd, 1981) is widely held to be an accurate depiction of the state of mind of British workers as the effects of the recession have pushed back their power in the labour market. **Richard Hyman**, in the updated version of the classic *Strikes* (Fontana, 1984), suggests that the early 1980s have been a period of 'coercive pacification', during which the economic and industrial policies of the government were 'intended to undermine workers' collective strength and confidence' (p. 199).

Since 1979 trade-union membership has been in decline, falling by 17 per cent by the end of 1984, and, apart from the large hiccup to the figures caused by the 1984/85 miners' strike, so too have the number of days lost through strike action (although see pp. 85–87 – *Employment Gazette*, (Department of Employment, January 1986). Escalating unemployment (hitting especially hard at those sectors of industry with traditionally high concentrations of union membership, such as certain manufacturing industries), privatisation of public enterprises and public expenditure cuts, have all conspired to undermine trade-union size. As Hyman suggests, perhaps most significant have been the three pieces of legislation affecting union power: the Employment Acts of 1980 and 1982 and the Trade Union Act of 1984. While the 1980 Act outlawed secondary picketing and the 1982 Act encouraged the introduction of secret ballots for closed shop arrangements, it is the 1984 Act that may have the most impact on trade-union prac-tices. This Act requires unions to hold secret ballots before taking strike action and during elections for executive posts. It ensures that trade unions with political funds vote regularly on whether money should be spent in this way.

Under these changed market conditions it is hardly surprising that some employers have taken the opportunity to restructure their industries. Research into telecommunications, the motor industry and electrical engineering shows that a shift in shop-floor power has taken place. Traditional working practices favouring the unions have been destroyed, the demarcation of jobs has been reduced and flexibility of the workforce increased. Often managements have attempted to bypass unions altogether by increasing the amount of direct contact with the shop floor by the use of 'quality circles' – small groups of between five and ten employees who work together and meet regularly to discuss and resolve job-related problems.

Some researchers argue, however, that in some industries trade-union power remains more intact than is suggested by reports about the spread of flexible working patterns. It may be too early to see any clear patterns emerging as British industry adopts methods 'After Japan'. This suggests the need for small, case-study surveys of different workplaces and industries (G. Salaman, *Working*, Ellis Horwood/Tavistock, 1986). At the same time, in recognition of the dynamic nature of industrial relations, Marxist and non-Marxist analysts alike have begun to look for an inter-grated theory of *conflict and co-operation at work*. As Richard Hyman suggests, 'to explain convincingly why there are so few strikes, or why disputes occur when and where they do, it is important to regard them not merely as incidents of industrial relations but as part of a continuum of practices and relationships inherent in any work situation' (*Strikes*, 1984, p. 184). As **P. K. Edwards** and **H. Scullion** (*The Social Organisation of Industrial Conflict*, Basil Blackwell, 1982) found in their study of seven British factories, different patterns of workers' relationships with one another and with management can assist or obstruct an awareness of their collective grievances and their expression in different forms of action. In sum, the organisation of work and different management strategies for securing control of the work-force were vitally important in determining the nature of conflict at work. In one factory they studied, high rates of labour turnover and employee absenteeism could be interpreted as a form of conflict. In another, such actions might not be a sign of this at all, but rather an expected part of the employment relationship at that factory and in that industry. They also suggest, therefore, that an adequate analysis of industrial relations and conflict must involve research at the level of working situation and environment, as well as the wider level of state and society. In short, they imply that an understanding of the labour process is essential in order to make sense of trends in work and the dynamics of industrial relations.

The sociology of (paid) work has been transformed by events of the last fifteen years – theoretically by Harry Braverman and LPT, and empirically by the changed economic climate. In the next chapter we shall look at research into one of the most dramatic of these changes: unemployment.

nployment

Introduction

Mass unemployment both affects and reflects the way in which work in society is organised, and has great significance for the individuals and communities affected by it. For this reason in recent years sociologists have viewed research into unemployment as a means of linking 'the personal troubles of milieu' to 'the public issue of social structure' (C. Wright Mills, *The Sociological Imagination*, Penguin Books, 1970, pp. 8–9). Sociologists have hoped to demonstrate the power of the sociological imagination through their research into the impact of unemployment, its unequal distribution among different social groups, and its costs for society as a whole. Yet it is questionable how successful they have been so far. Between 1979 and 1982 unemployment doubled to just under 3 million without there being any major disruption of the social fabric. A discernible shift in the level of unemployment which is publicly acceptable has taken place. There appears to be considerable acceptance of certain myths about unemployment and the unemployed: that many unemployed people are 'better off on the dole'; that nobody suffers, as people did in the thirties; that many are 'scroungers' and 'work-shy'; that a considerable number work 'off the books' in the *black economy* at the same time as signing on; and that the unemployment problem is either a product of a world-wide crisis, and therefore no government could possibly manage it any better than the present one, or is so complex a problem that it cannot be understood properly, but only suffered. Of course, this is where social science comes in. The theories of economic change outlined in Chapter 2 are all attempts to explain what has been going on in Western economies. If the detail and range of the theories has not been fully aired in public debate then this is a cause of concern for sociologists, but it is also a sobering reminder of the relationship between the social sciences and the policy-making process. Sociologist do not make policy; at best their research can be used to *inform* debates about policy. Why, then, have they been unable to get their ideas and research evidence across? This would be an interesting study in the sociology of knowledge.

Part of the answer probably lies with the impact of unemployment on the population as a whole. As Lord David Ivor Young, the Employment Secretary, is reported to have remarked in June 1986, 'For the 87 per cent in work, the country has never had as good a time as it has today.' Despite the scorn with which this comment was received by critics of the government, there was more than a grain of truth in it. Unemployment is unequally distributed throughout the population, and thus the direct financial costs of it are only borne by a small proportion of society. For those who remain in secure, full-time work, the standard of living has continued to increase, as it did in the 1930s. As these quotations from the middle-class unemployed reveal, people fail to appreciate the nature of unemployment until it happens to them:

> People expect you to feel the way they *think* they would feel if they were out of a job. . . . I get the feeling that people think I could get a job if I really tried – and I now find myself wondering if this is true.

> Those who've never been out of work can have no idea what it's like – that's why it's so easy to pontificate about what's good for the country.
>   (S. Fineman, *White Collar Unemployment*, John Wiley & Sons, 1983, p. 113)

Alternatively, as a Marxist might argue, perhaps it is a classic case of 'false consciousness', induced by a right-wing press, subservient broadcasting media and supported by the actions of a state apparatus geared toward the maintenance and reproduction of the capitalist status quo. We will not resolve this question here, however. In the space that we have available we can only indicate some of the areas of research which have been conducted which demonstrate the 'mythical' nature of the assumptions listed above. Firstly, we shall consider the 'numbers game': the definition and measurement of unemployment and its distribution. Secondly, we will consider research into the impact of unemployment: its costs for individuals and society and especially how it is related to poverty and inequality. Finally, as a means of assessing different theories of unemployment, we shall provide a case study of youth unemployment in contemporary Britain.

Counting the unemployed

Unemployment became politically sensitive in Britain in the late 1970s. The Conservative Party used an advertising agency, Saatchi and Saatchi, to devise a series of slick political advertisements for display on roadside hoardings and in cinemas pointing out the failings of the Labour government: 'Labour isn't working', ran the slogan under a never-ending queue winding its way out of the benefit office. In 1979, just before Mrs Thatcher formed her first administration, people were dismayed by the official unemployment percentage of 5.6 per cent – around 1.4 million. But this figure was well known by social scientists to be an under-estimation, particularly of women who were not registered as unemployed, but who would have liked a paid job if one had been available.

No government agency in the world produces totally sociologically satisfactory unemployment statistics. But as with many other areas of social life sociologists interested in unemployment cannot ignore the evidence provided by official statistics. It is important to know how they are produced in order to be able to interpret them.

Unemployment figures are no more than 'snapshots' of *stocks and flows* into and out of unemployment which are subject to seasonal variation. The Department of Employment therefore gives actual and seasonally adjusted figures in order to be able to estimate long-term trends as accurately as possible. Over the last ten years, the *inflow rate* into unemployment has grown massively, whereas the *outflow rate* has remained stable or fallen. As the size of the unemployed *stock* has increased, so too has the average duration of unemployment. By March 1986, 1.4 million, or 40 per cent, of the unemployed had been without work for twelve months or more (the *long-term unemployed*). In 1976, a figure of 200,000 had caused an outcry.

In October 1982 the government made the first of several alterations to the way in which the unemployment figures were officially calculated: only people *claiming* unemployment or supplementary benefit were to be included in the count as unemployed. This method of counting the unemployed is unsatisfactory as it is especially open to political and administrative manipulation. If you can cut the number of claimants – for example, by making the process of claiming entitlements more stringent – you can cut the unemployment figures. This appears to be what the government is doing with the 'available for work' forms introduced into unemployment benefit offices in the autumn of 1986. The government has also recently altered the way in which the unemployment rate (percentage) is calculated. Previously the number of unemployed were expressed as a percentage of the latest mid-year estimate of *all employees in employment* plus the unemployed at the same date. Since July 1986 the denominator has been the *employed labour force*, which contains members of HM Forces, and an estimate, as there are no accurate figures, for the number of self-employed. This not only *increased* the size of the working population at a stroke, it also *reduced* the unemployment rate – for example, in April 1986, from 13.6 per cent, on the old basis, to 12.1 per cent on the new.

Support for the changes has come from those who have claimed that the official unemployment figures were artificially inflated. It has been claimed that many of those counted as unemployed, such as the mentally and physically ill, are 'unemployable'; that school leavers should be subtracted from the monthly totals; that many of the registered unemployed are not actually looking for work, or already have a job and use unemployment benefit as a supplementary source of income; and that the changes are necessary to help bring Britain in line with other countries. In November 1983, when the official unemployment total was 3,094,000, the *Sunday Times* published a table which showed that if these criticisms were acted upon the 'real' unemployed figure would be 1.4 million less. Public disillusionment with unemployment statistics has been fed by observations made by top-ranking politicians and industrialists about 'scroungers', living it up 'on the dole'. In October 1985 Sir Michael Edwardes, former chairman of British Leyland, Jeffrey Archer, former vice-chairman of the Conservative Party and Lord Young, the Employment Secretary, all made widely publicised claims (reported in the *Guardian* on 15 and 31 October 1985) with the implication that there were perhaps nearly 1 million scroungers, either working 'off the books' in the *black economy*, or not really looking for work at all, who featured in the figures.

The social science community has research evidence which provides counter arguments to these ideas, however. The number of *unregistered* unemployed has been known to be huge for many years. A large proportion of women failed to register for employment in the 1970s as they had little confidence in the job agencies' ability to find work for them (see Chapter 7, pp. 83–5). The notion of employability actually fluctuates with the state of demand in the economy – so the argument about 'unemployables' inflating the figures is a crude one. Since November 1980 school leavers have been barred from claiming benefit until September each year. So, together with the change in the monthly count of unemployment to claimants only in October 1982, the monthly totals for June, July and August are now estimated to 'lose' regularly between 100,000 and 200,000 unemployed school leavers who are not yet eligible to sign on. Finally, the research evidence which exists about work in the black economy suggests quite a different picture from the one provided by anecdotes and stories in the press. Such activity is much less likely to be carried out by the unemployed than people in full-time work (S. Smith, *Britain's Shadow Economy*, Oxford University Press, 1986, and Reading 8.7, pp. 103–4).

Although various official and independent surveys have revealed that the unemployed experience a considerable drop in their living standards – that unemployment hurts – it is clear that the myths about it continue to sustain the general belief that things are not really so bad. Social science research, therefore, has an important role in revealing the true extent of the social distribution of unemployment. We will consider some of this research in more detail in the next section.

The social distribution of unemployment

Whatever the problems with the accuracy of the data, it is quite clear that there are considerable regional and social differences in the incidence of unemployment. Various accounts are available which discuss its unequal distribution across regions, occupations, industries and among different social groups (Adrian Sinfield, *What Unemployment Means*, Martin Robertson, 1981; A. Sinfield and B. Showler (eds), *The Workless State*, Martin Robertson, 1981;

D. Thomas, 'Taking the measure of unemployemnt', in *New Society*, 16 May 1985). Northern Ireland has remained the worst affected region: its average unemployment rate in 1984 was just under 21 per cent, compared with a UK average of about 13 per cent. Unemployment also varies within regions: in Scotland, for example (average rate 15.1 per cent), unemployment in April 1986 ranged from 18.7 per cent in the Strathclyde region to 5.7 per cent on the Shetland Islands (*Social Trends*, No. 16, HMSO, 1986; *Employment Gazette*, Department of Employment, June 1986). Aside from regional differences, it is the unequal burden of high unemployment on different social groups which has attracted the comments of official and independent researchers alike. **A. Sinfield** provides a good summary of their findings: 'those most likely to be unemployed are people in low-paying and insecure jobs, the very young and the oldest in the labour force, people from ethnic or racial minorities, people from among the disabled and handicapped, and generally those with the least skills and living in the most depressed areas' (*What Unemployment Means*).

Table 5.1 shows that, for men, unemployment has been

Table 5.1   Unemployment by socio-economic group and sex, GB, 1982 (per cent)

Socio-economic group	Men		Women	
	Working population	Unemployed population	Working population	Unemployed population
Professional	6	2	1	0
Employers/ managers	18	6	6	5
Intermediate non-manual	9	4	18	6
Junior non-manual	8	5	37	32
Skilled manual	41	43	7	7
Semi-skilled/ personal service	15	26	23	42
Unskilled manual	3	15	8	7
n =	6287	777	4437	394

Source: D. N. Ashton, *Unemployment under Capitalism*, Wheatsheaf Books, 1986, p. 51.

concentrated in the semi-skilled and unskilled manual socio-economic groups, whereas for women groups especially at risk are the semi-skilled and personal service workers. As we pointed out in Chapter 2, the latest research into racial disadvantage has shown that black people in Britain are almost twice as likely to be unemployed as whites. What is it about these groups that makes them so susceptible to unemployment? A recent attempt to explain the social distribution of unemployment is provided by **D. N. Ashton** in *Unemployment under Capitalism*.

Ashton argues that the pattern of unemployment in society stems from the *institutional regulation* of the labour market, rather than the personal characteristics of (would-be) workers. The idea of a *free market for labour* is largely a myth. The labour market in the real world is made up of *segments* and *shelters*, which restrict the mobility of workers between types and areas of employment. Largely the product of employers' recruitment procedures, workers rarely move between different *segments*. However, some groups of workers have been able to maximise their job security by obtaining protection from arbitrary dismissal and loss of work through fluctuations in the demand for their labour. These *labour market shelters* offer differing degrees of protection in the midst of the economic recession to different occupational groups. Access to shelters depends less on personal characteristics than on certi-fication and employers' needs. Ashton thus agrees with the find-ings of S. Bowles and H. Gintis (*Schooling in Capitalist America*, Routledge & Kegan Paul, 1976) that an individual's social origins are linked to their occupational destinations through the school system. People from lower working-class families tend to encounter problems with the culture of the school, perform worse than their middle-class peers, and hence enter lower occupational segments, offering fewer shelters. Children from the middle class adapt better to school, and go on to obtain forms of certification necessary for entry into the professions and more sheltered occu-pations. The process is not as determinate as it looks – reliance on educational certification permits a degree of fluidity – and some working-class children do 'make it', while some middle-class kids do not. With respect to the position of black people in the British labour market, Ashton argues that their failure results from the existence of racist beliefs about their inferiority as a social group. As racism structures their work experience, black people's position in the labour market is doubly determined. Blacks were used to fill the least desirable jobs when the white population vacated them. Once in poorly paid jobs, with bad working conditions and insecure incomes, *institutionalised racism* has kept them there, creating a vicious circle: low-paid work – bad social conditions – poor educational performance – entry into 'secondary' employment. The situation is well documented in P. Braham *et al.* (eds), *Discrimination and Disadvantage in Employment* (Harper and Row, 1981) as well as the latest Policy Studies Institute survey. In short, Ashton argues that it is mechanisms in the British labour market which are responsible for the particular shape and distribution of unemployment in the 1980s. It is an argument which makes much sense of the data. It is also compatible with the view of the employment relationship as a power relation. However, in order to find out about the costs and experience of unemployment in the 1980s we have to turn to other research.

The costs and experience of unemployment

The Department of Health and Social Security (DHSS) has investigated the *financial effect* of unemployment on men in families by comparing incomes in and out of work in 1978 and 1982. The relationship between incomes when out of work to incomes when in work is called the *replacement ratio*. In 1978, 30 per cent of the sample had replacement ratios of under 50 per cent; their incomes when out of work were less than *half* what they would have earned if they had been in work. Only 4 per cent of the sample were actually better off on the dole – that is, had replacement ratios of over 100 per cent. Many of these had begun to receive their occupational pension when they became unemployed, and it was this which had boosted their out-of-work income. By 1982 the number of men receiving less than half what they would have earned in paid work had grown to 39 per cent of the sample. The number who were better off had fallen to 3 per cent (*Social Trends*, 16, HMSO, 1986, p. 83). Thus there is official confirmation that the unemployed have become increasingly financially worse off, in comparison with the waged, as the recession has worsened. Sociological surveys, such as **Peter Townsend**'s comprehensive study of *Poverty in the United Kingdom* (1979, pp. 589–617), have consistently demonstrated a strong correlation between unemployment and poverty.

Research carried out in the 1930s has remained influential in terms of understanding the *psychological* effects of unemployment (M. Jahoda *et al.*, *Marienthal: the Sociography of an Unemployed Community*, Tavistock, 1972). The notion that people go through a series of *stages* when adjusting to their new unemployed situation – shock and immobilisation, recovery and optimism, creeping self-doubt and pessimism, and adaptation and the adoption of a new identity – has become something of an axiom in psychological studies of the unemployed. Recently, however, the model of stages has been challenged.

A series of articles on 'occupationless health' in the *British Medical Journal* (12 October to 14 December 1985, and 25 January to 15 February 1986) featured the latest research evidence on the connection between unemployment and *ill-health*. The research suggests that the unemployed die earlier, especially by suicide, and suffer more physical and mental ill-health than people in work (J. Laurence, 'Unemployment: health hazards', in *New Society*, 21 March 1986, pp. 492–4). It is not actually proven that unemployment *causes* ill-health, but, as Laurence writes, 'the circumstantial evidence is strong'. Most research points to the absence of a *steady income* as a major factor. In fact **Peter Kelvin** and **Joanna E. Jarrett** (*Unemployment: Its Social Psychological Effects*, Cambridge University Press, 1985) suggest that the social psychological effects of unemployment are, at present, indistinguishable from the effects of *poverty*. They argue that researchers have been too quick to adopt the model of stages without really testing it. The reactions which have been treated as stemming from unemployment could just as likely be responses to falling income. Many normal activities, not directly related to unemployment, become impossible without adequate funds. Kelvin and Jarrett suggest that in everyday life there is a 'norm of reciprocity', which insufficient income make it impossible to sustain. The *social isolation* of unemployment, often explained in terms of a loss of workplace contacts, 'stigmatisation' and withdrawal, may be due to the more *material* factor of poverty. This idea is in line with those of sociologists who have criticised psychological orthodoxy for tending to treat people as passive subjects and thus for obscuring the great *diversity of responses* to unemployment. As Adrian Sinfield has suggested in *What Unemployment Means*, types of response to unemployment and the duration of each phase will depend upon *previous experience and expectations*. Unemployment will affect people differently depending on their economic circumstances, alternative sources of self-esteem and activity, and the values and expectations of the *subculture* and *reference groups* to which they belong. The effects of unemployment on health are also likely to vary from one social group to another. The middle-class male may be more likely to contemplate suicide, whereas the low wage earner faces an intensification of existing problems.

In order to gather evidence about the different meanings that the experience of unemployment has for different social groups, qualitative research techniques, such as unstructured and semi-structured interviews and oral history accounts, have been used by sociologists and writers. Such methods are seen as invaluable for tapping the effects of unemployment on the individual, their families and whole communities (D. Marsden, *Workless*, Croom Helm, 1982; J. Seabrook, *Unemployment*, Quartet Books, 1982; S. Fineman, *White Collar Unemployment*, John Wiley and Sons, 1983; C. D. Wallace and R. E. Pahl, 'Polarisation, unemployment and all forms of work' in S. Allen *et al.* (eds), *The Experience of Unemployment*, Macmillan, 1986). What stands out in many of these studies is the centrality of the *wage* as the chief source of status, as well as livelihood, in capitalist society. Owing to their socialisation and life experiences, most people – including women, who previously have been ignored by researchers (A. Coyle, *Redundant Women*, Women's Press, 1984) – now perceive the *need for work* as the *need for employment* (M. Jahoda, *Employment and Unemployment*, Cambridge University Press; 1982, pp. 83–4). Without a wage, the unemployed experience forms of social and cultural *exclusion*. This has been observed particularly in studies of the young unemployed (*The Social Condition of Young People in Wolverhampton in 1984* (Wolverhampton Youth Review, Wolverhampton Borough Council, June 1985). As Paul Willis, research co-ordinator of the Wolverhampton project, argues:

[There is] . . . a vast urban swathe of young people who are excluded from the things the rest of us take for granted or which are the common objects of desire. The unemployed are in poverty compared to the rest of us. They cannot do the things which the rest of society – orchestrated by consumerism and advertising – is geared to and always promoting. This is poverty in a cultural sense as well as in an economic sense.

(*Youth Unemployment and the New Poverty: a Summary of a Local Authority Review*, Wolverhampton Borough Council, 1985)

In the final section of this chapter we will consider some of the explanations for youth unemployment.

Youth unemployment

As noted in Chapter 2, youth unemployment has grown greatly in Britain in the last ten years. Its persistence has produced a number of explanations, some of which have figured prominently in the public debate about the problem. Much attention has been paid to *demographic changes*; it has been argued that the problem has been caused by greater numbers of young people offering themselves on the labour market. Another argument has been that young people have priced themselves out of jobs. Others have suggested that young people have lacked the skills, training and technical education to match the needs of employers. Put together, these views have led to an argument for more *vocationalism* in education – that is, the need for greater emphasis upon training in technical skills and upon linking school more closely to working life.

The Manpower Services Commission (MSC), a quasi-autonomous body responsible to the Employment minister, has been used as the vehicle for repairing the apparent damage. Though initially involved only in 'propping up' unemployed, unqualified youth in the 1970s, through job creation and work experience programmes and then the Youth Opportunities Programme (YOP), with the continued growth of youth unemployment in the 1980s, the MSC has been given the role of administering and developing a strategy for changing the entry of young people into the labour market via the Youth Training Scheme (YTS) and the Technical and Vocational Education Initiative (TVEI). Both schemes, it is argued, mark the start of a new relationship between school and work for *all* school leavers. A sign of the significance of the youth unemployment situation in Britain is that approximately half of the MSC budget in 1986 was devoted to measures on behalf of youth.

Such explanations of youth unemployment and the government's response have not passed without criticism. It has been argued that there is an inherent tendency for 'supply side' employment policies in the labour market to *blame the victim* for being unemployed. Certainly, if one starts from the view that unemployment is the responsibility of *individuals* one gets a different set of policies than if one sees it as the product of *structural and institutional factors*. Thus training is conceived as a kind of solution to unemployment, supporting the notion that there are jobs waiting for those who are suitably trained or willing to take them. What evidence is there that youth unemployment *is* a product of structural and institutional factors?

Firstly, changes in the supply of labour have only been a contributory factor, and not a cause, of high youth unemployment. The growth in the numbers of young people offering themselves on the labour market peaked in 1979, before the onset of very high levels of unemployment (D.N. Ashton, *Unemployment under Capitalism*, p. 108). Secondly, there is little support for the view that young people have been pricing themselves out of work. There is evidence that young people have high expectations about what work could offer them, including unrealistic ideas about the wages they could expect, but there is no evidence that high wages have been to blame for young people's unemployment. Instead, many reports point to the continued use of young people as cheap and easily disposable labour in some industries (C. Pond, 'Youth unemployment – are wages to blame?' in *Low Pay Review*, No. 8, February 1982). Thirdly – and this is the focus for the bulk of sociological writing – many commentators on youth unemployment are cynical about the purposes of the 'new vocationalism'.

For Marxists, such as **Andy Friend** and **Andy Metcalf** (*Slump City: the Politics of Mass Unemployment*, Pluto Press, 1981), unemployment reveals the unequal nature of modern capitalist societies and the processes by which inequality is reproduced. There are two distinctive features of their argument. Firstly, capitalism is seen as an inherently unstable economic system. Capitalist economies therefore require *surplus populations* which in times of economic prosperity – such as in the period after World War II – can be recruited to meet the need for labour. In the UK this need was met by immigration in the 1950s and 1960s and the increased use of female labour. When economic growth gave way to recession these groups became surplus again and have been marginalised by immigration controls and discrimination based upon sexual and ethnic differences. Secondly, Marxists view the state as a *capitalist state*. The state acts in such a way as to sustain and reproduce society as the economy is restructured. This is particularly apparent in the way the state is dealing with unemployed youth.

As we have seen earlier, the Marxist argument is very powerful, but it requires amending if we want to take account of such issues as women's position in the 'surplus population'. Women in different parts of the occupational structure, in different *labour market segments*, are treated differently. They are not all members of the 'reserve army of labour'. Marxist writers who have recognised the problems with some of the old formulations have produced some very interesting analyses of recent developments in education and training. A good illustration is **Inge Bates** *et al.*, *Schooling for the Dole* (Macmillan, 1984). The authors analyse different aspects of the recent changes introduced by the MSC. The overall argument of the book is that the new vocationalism is a response to three needs:

1 for the government to be seen to be doing something about youth unemployment;
2 in times of economic crisis for certain attitudes to be fostered among young people to ensure that they will remain keen to join the labour force, while accepting their fate as unemployed;
3 for the government to place the blame on the school system and young people themselves, rather than the government's political decisions affecting the state of the economy or the failings of the market system.

Although in summary form the argument sounds rather functionalist and conspiratorial, the various writers in the book make it clear that they view the outcome of the current social and economic climate as far from certain.

Another analysis of unemployment which utilises the notion of 'labour market segmentation' though not written from a Marxist perspective, is the recent work of D. N. Ashton. He suggests that it is the 'institutional regulation' of the labour markets in different countries which explains the varied patterns of youth unemployment in the advanced capitalist countries (see Table 2.2, p. 16). In the 1960s and early 1970s in Britain many fifteen- and sixteen-year-old school leavers (those who were the least qualified) obtained work easily, but in the late 1970s, with only a small secondary and unregulated sector of the labour market, such young people increasingly found it difficult to get jobs. As a result, youth unemployment in Britain has been very responsive to changes in the level of *aggregate demand* – that is, to the general health of the economy. Ashton cites research which suggests that for every 1 per cent increase in male unemployment, the youth rate rose by 1.7 per cent in the 1970s. Young people are also adversely affected precisely because they are *new recruits*. In a recession, the first thing that employers reduce is the amount of new labour they take on. Ashton recognises, however, that changes in the occupational structure have also affected the employment opportunities of young people. In particular, their opportunities have been affected by the following factors:

1   the decline in the number of unskilled jobs in manufacturing industry which previously took on untrained labour (such as 'the lads' in P. Willis, *Learning to Labour*, 1977);
2   the fact that employers in Britain tend to recruit women, especially married women, for those kinds of part-time jobs which have been created in the service sector in the 1980s; and
3   jobs such as clerical and typing in commerce, which previously provided work for the school leaver, are being transformed by the new office technology.

In sum, Ashton argues that an adequate explanation of youth unemployment must take into account changes at work in the structure of the labour market which are reducing the points of entry into work for young people.

The suggestion that in order to explain youth unemployment properly we need to examine contemporary changes in the labour process is echoed by **Paul Thompson**. ('The new vocationalism: the Trojan horse of the MSC', in *The Social Science Teacher*, vol. 13, No. 2, pp. 47–9).He argues that the new vocationalism marks a new stage in the 'restructuring of education in the image of the capitalist labour process', rather than any great advance in the education and training of young people. In a similar vein to Bates *et al.*, Thompson interprets the MSC training schemes as a response by the state to economic restructuring, but he emphasises the link with the labour process. The aim of the YTS is to produce a pool of semi-skilled workers, prepared to receive low wages, in a newly restructured labour market for youth. Contrary to the arguments of writers like Bowles and Gintis and Althusser, Thompson argues that in Britain, until recently, a precise *correspondence* between the education system and the needs of the economy did not exist. The education system in the past may have acted as a 'general filter' into the labour market. But what the YTS and TVEI promise to do is to train young people *directly* for work. The YTS is a means of attuning young people to the new conditions which await them in work. The state has responded to economic restructuring by attempting to gain greater control over the young working class. Of course this need not mean that the state is successful in its aim. The Special Employment Measures implemented by the MSC do not gain overwhelming support from young people. Many YTS entrants have been critical of the low pay and poor training offered. According to Youthaid, the independent youth employment charity, between September 1983 and April 1986 fewer than six out of ten YTS leavers got work, and nearly one in three joined the dole queues (Youthaid, *Leave it Out – Young People Leaving the Youth Training Scheme 1983–1986*, 1986). And increasingly there is evidence that the YTS has been racist and sexist in its operation, sustaining discrimination and bias in the labour market (S. Ollerearnshaw, 'How blacks lose out on the YTS', *New Society*, 16 May 1986; C. Cockburn, *Training for Her Job and for His*, Equal Opportunities Commission, 1986). In many ways what happens to young people will depend on what they *themselves* demand. Although some researchers have suggested that they may be turning their attention to leisure as a 'central life interest' – the video arcade in the 1980s replacing the billiard hall and the street of the 1930s as the hangout for young people with time on their hands – for the majority of young people, paid work, or at least the income that goes with it, remains a priority.

6 Sociology, work and the future

The future of work

With the dramatic decline in employment in the advanced capitalist countries sociologists, among others, have begun to turn
their attention to questions left aside since the last great depression
in the 1930s. Apart from the nature, causes and impact of
unemployment the implicit meanings of such previously
unambiguous terms as 'work', 'employment', even 'leisure', are
being inspected as they are in the process of being changed and
challenged. As Professor Ray Pahl has recently written, 'a society
that falters when referring to something apparently so basic to
human existence is likely to be changing in a fundamental way'
(*Divisions of Labour*, Basil Blackwell, 1984, p. 17). Some writers
have speculated recently that we are witnessing the demise of the
work ethic and suffering from the impact of a 'leisure shock'.
Underpinning much of this thinking lies the notion, first spelled
out in detail by Professor **Daniel Bell** (*The Coming of Post-
industrial Society: a Venture in Social Forecasting*, Penguin Books,
1974), that we are living in a *post-industrial society* dominated by
professional, service and scientific work. With the development
of information technology the idea has been given a new lease of
life. Some now see an *information society* developing out of post-
industrialism. A former Marxist, **André Gorz**, has written two
books (*Farewell to the Working Class*, Pluto Press, 1982 and *Paths
to Paradise: on the Liberation from Work*, Pluto Press, 1985) which
develop this idea. Gorz suggests that the new technology is abol-
ishing work as it has been known. As a result, the manual
working class (the classical proletariat) are no longer important
to the socialist project and work is no longer central as an arena
of contestation and struggle. Instead, Gorz argues that what is
required is a redistribution of time and leisure. The possibilities
for a society of leisure are within reach. This is an interesting
thesis, which has provoked much debate. But how far are we

living in a 'post-industrial society', in which work is losing its importance?

Most research evidence generated by sociologists simply does not support 'post-industrialism' (K. Kumar, *Prophecy and Progress*, Penguin Books, 1978; D. Lyon, 'From "post-industrialism" to "information society": a new social transformation?' in *Sociology*, vol. 20, No. 4, Nov. 1986). The decline of manufacturing employment in the advanced industrial capitalist societies of the West has been too readily interpreted as a sign of the decline of the importance of work and a fundamental transformation of society in general. As we have seen, manufacturing employment ought not to be taken as representative of all forms of work. Additionally, it is ethnocentric to talk about the 'decline of manufacturing', when simply what has happened is that manufacturing employment has been relocated to other parts of the globe. Although the last two decades of the twentieth century promise substantial changes in patterns of employment, technology, the role of the state and so on, these in themselves will not signify a change in the capitalist socio-economic structure. It is clear that within the advanced capitalist societies paid employment will remain centrally important and will continue to be so for the foreseeable future. Employment provides, for better or for worse, the solution to three vital personal issues under the market system: it provides a means by which people occupy their time; it provides a status related to their main social role; and it gives them access to an income. As we have seen, unemployment does not provide a satisfactory resolution to these issues.

Sociology and the future of work

Professor **Richard Brown** has recently written that sociologists studying work in the future will need to consider carefully four areas of research ('Working on work', in *Sociology*, vol. 18, No. 3, Aug. 1984). They will have to reconceptualise what they understand by 'work'. The 'work = paid employment' equation ignores much work carried out by women and unduly restricts the scope of the subject. Sociologists also need to consider the historical development of the present divisions of labour, sexual as well as technical, and the influence of different managerial and trade union traditions on the present system of industrial relations. The way in which people's attitudes towards work are socially created, and how the workforce is daily and generationally reproduced through institutions such as the state, the education and training system and the family, all require investigation. And, finally, sociologists of work need to broaden their horizons in order to understand fully the contemporary role of trans-national corporations, the international division of labour and the migration of workers, in shaping the spatial distribution of work on a global scale. A sociology of work which fully addressed these issues would be very impressive!

The question of the future of work and what is to be done about the current situation is, of course, a deeply political matter. The role of the sociologist, Brown suggests, is to contribute to the discussion by revealing 'the conditions of our present plight', developing 'alternative futures' and 'exploring the conditions necessary for their realisation'. **Tony Watts** has recently outlined four *scenarios* of possible alternative futures for work:

> If the political decision is to let narrow economic forces prevail, this means that unemployment is unlikely to be significantly reduced and may well grow. . . . It is possible . . . that those outside employment, instead of being stigmatised, could form the basis of a new leisure class. Alternatively, it is possible that ways could be found of distributing employment, and the income and status associated with it, more evenly. A further alternative is that the concept of work could be broadened beyond that of employment, and that greater value could be attached to self-employment and to forms of work outside the formal economy. . . . We will term them (a) the unemployment scenario, (b) the leisure scenario, (c) the employment scenario, and (d) the work scenario.
>
> (*Education, Unemployment and the Future of Work*, Open University Press, 1983, pp. 100–1)

Watts suggests that the first and second scenarios are most inegalitarian; they are likely to lead to greater social divisions between the 'haves' and the 'have-nots', even if the stigma of accepting low-level benefits were removed from those people not involved in the employment system. The employment and work scenarios could also lead to inequalities of wealth, but at least they hold out the possibility that people could have some say in the type of socio-economic policies pursued by government.

As is obvious, these scenarios involve judgements of value, and ultimately only political actions could bring about any of the desired changes. Where does sociology fit in? It is a subject which asks penetrating questions about society, often revealing matters which those who do well out of the existing state of affairs would rather not have revealed. Sociology is, moreover, a *disciplined* way of generating information and producing theories about social affairs. Its findings are open to discussion and debate. The state of knowledge in the subject is in this sense always open to later revision. It can contribute best under social conditions where free, wide-ranging, popular debate over important matters is possible and permissible. It is to be hoped that such conditions prevail in the future, and that the sociological imagination can continue to be brought to bear on the topics looked at in this book, some of the most pressing questions of our time.

PART 3

Statistical data and documentary readings

7 Statistical data

In this chapter we shall provide up-to-date statistical information on the world of work, employment and unemployment. There are sections on the labour force, the sexual division of labour, rewards and deprivations at work, the social construction of official labour statistics, using unemployment and strikes as our examples, sexism in statistics and the household division of labour. First, some remarks are provided about sources of data.

Sources of data

The main sources of data for sociologists interested in work, employment and unemployment are official statistics compiled by government departments. The Department of Employment (DE) publishes figures on employment, unemployment vacancies notified to Job Centres, industrial disputes, earnings, wage rates, hours of work and labour costs in the *Employment Gazette*, published monthly. Detailed analyses and comparisons are published annually in *Social Trends* from such surveys as the *Census of Employment*, *New Earnings Survey* and the *Labour Force Survey*.

All these sources suffer from the drawback that they are largely confined to *registered* employment and unemployment, although the actual number of 'hidden' equivalents is considered to be quite large. Official statistics are concerned with employment as *productive activity* which enters directly into national accounts – economic activity – whereas sociological interest is much wider, including forms of work *outside* employment. This emphasis on

productive labour in official statistics can lead to a mail-order cata-
logue agent, a childminder or a cleaner who considers herself
primarily a housewife, being categorised as 'economically
inactive'. Despite the problems, however, it is difficult to envisage
a drastic overhaul of the system of data collection. As they stand,
official statistics do enable researchers to make important general
statements about the importance of work in the British social
structure.

The labour force

The DE uses different measures of employment in different
contexts. For example, 'employees in employment' refers to all
civilian employees insured under the National Insurance Acts and
benefit claimants registered as unemployed, whereas the
'employed labour force' or 'working population' includes an
estimate for the self-employed and HM Forces as well as
employees in employment. The term 'labour force' is most often
used to describe those people who are 'economically active':
employees in work, the self-employed and the registered
unemployed.

Despite the conviction with which government ministers quote
employment figures, their basis is remarkably flimsy. As with
unemployment statistics, the calculation of employees in employment has undergone several changes in recent years. Calculations

Table 7.1 The UK labour force, June 1985[1]

Category in labour force	Numbers (000)	Percentage[2]
Male employees	11,764	42.9
Female employees	9,528	34.75
Self-employed	2,620	9.56
Armed Forces	326	1.19
Unemployed	3,179	11.6
Total	27,417	100.00

1 Unadjusted for seasonal variation.
2 Percentages for total labour force including the unemployed.

Source: *Employment Gazette*, Nov. 1985.

for the increases in the number of the self-employed in recent years are in fact no more than projections based upon the assumption that the rate of change between 1981 and 1985 is continuing. Until 1986 the estimated number of self-employed people was left out of the mid-year calculation of the labour force, partly because of this lack of precision. In sum, changes in employment recorded between one quarter and the next in any one year tell us far less about the success or otherwise of government economic policy than is often supposed. Nevertheless, Table 7.1 shows the latest available estimate.

Occupational classifications and distribution of the workforce

During the last 140 years – the time which detailed, fairly reliable statistics have been available – the absolute size of the economically active population has grown from under 7 million in Great Britain in 1841 to over 25 million in 1981. Since the mid-twentieth century the increased proportion of women in employment, and especially of married women, has more than offset the declining proportion of adult men who are economically active. Growth in the labour force between 1971 and 1985 of 1.7 million is entirely attributable to women, whereas over the same period the male labour force remained relatively stable at around 15.5 million in total.

The industrial distribution of the labour force shows considerable change over the same period. In 1851 22 per cent of the economically active population were engaged in agriculture, forestry and fishing; by 1911 this proportion had fallen to under 8 per cent and by 1971 to less than 2 per cent. The proportion in manufacturing industry (including gas, electricity and water) remained fairly constant in these three years: 40 per cent, nearly 35 per cent and nearly 40 per cent respectively. The major growth has been in the 'service industries', from 29 per cent in 1851, to 45 per cent in 1911 and 51 per cent in 1971.

The major changes which have taken place in the UK in the last twenty-five years are shown in Table 7.2. The most striking and relatively sudden decline is in the number and proportion of people employed in manufacturing industry, which occurred in

Table 7.2   UK employees in employment: by industry 1961–81, and by sex 1981 (thousands)

Employment category	1961 Total	1971 Total	1981 Total	1981 Male	%	1981 Female	%	1981 totals as % of all employees
Agriculture, forestry, fishing	710	432	360	270	2.2	89	1.0	1.6
Mining and quarrying	727	396	332	316	2.6	16	0.2	1.6
Manufacturing:								
food, drink, tobacco	793	770	632	385	3.1	247	2.8	
chemicals, coal, petroleum products	499	482	432	320	2.6	113	1.3	
metal manufacture	643	557	326	290	2.4	36	0.4	
engineering and allied industries	3,654	3,615	2,739	2,171	17.7	568	6.4	
textiles, leather, clothing	1,444	1,124	707	291	2.4	417	4.7	
rest of manufacturing	1,508	1,511	1,202	873	7.1	329	3.7	
TOTAL MANUFACTURING	8,540	8,058	6,038	4,330	35.3	1,709	19.1	28.5
Construction	1,485	1,262	1,132	1,023	8.3	109	1.2	5.3
Gas, electricity, water	389	377	340	272	2.2	68	0.8	1.6
Services								
transport and communication	1,678	1,568	1,440	1,164	9.5	276	3.1	
distributive trades	2,767	2,610	2,635	1,180	9.6	1,455	16.3	
insurance, banking, finance	684	976	1,233	577	4.7	656	7.3	
professional and scientific	2,124	2,989	3,695	1,161	9.4	2,533	28.4	
miscellaneous	1,819	1,946	2,414	1,017	8.3	1,397	15.6	
public administration	1,311	1,509	1,579	954	7.8	625	7.0	
TOTAL SERVICES	10,382	11,597	12,996	6,053	49.6	6,942	78.3	61.3
ALL INDUSTRIES AND SERVICES	22,233	22,122	21,198	12,264	100.0	8,934	100.0	100.0

Source: Social Trends, 13, 1983, p. 54.

the 1970s. The fall has continued since 1981; in August 1986 it was estimated that there were just 5,320,000 employees in British manufacturing industry, representing less than a quarter of all employees, and 115,000 fewer than in August 1985 (*Labour Research*, vol. 75, No. 11, Nov. 1986).

The sexual division of labour

The most enduring division between workers, employed or not, is the sexual division of labour. In virtually all societies sociologists and anthropologists have observed a division of work along gender lines, although the tasks carried out by each gender have varied considerably, making it difficult to argue for universal characteristics or aptitudes of men and women. Despite equal pay and sex discrimination legislation to promote equal opportunities, the labour market in Britain is characterised by occupational segregation by gender. Table 7.2 also shows the very different distribution of men and women throughout the labour force in 1981.

Questions (Table 7.2)

1   In terms of numbers in employment, which industry declined the most and which increased the most between 1961 and 1981?
2   Which were the most 'female' industries in 1981 in (a) manufacturing and (b) services?

Rewards and deprivations

Much sociological concern with work has been about the world of paid employment as a world of inequality of pay and conditions. Tables 7.3 and 7.4 provide information which supports such a view.

1   Pay and hours

Table 7.3 shows different levels of pay and hours by manual and non-manual men and women, data for which was collected

Table 7.3 Levels of pay and hours, April 1985, GB[1]

	Male			Female			ALL
	Manual	Non-manual	All	Manual	Non-manual	All	
Average gross weekly earnings (£) of which:	163.6	225.0	192.4	101.3	133.8	126.4	171.0
overtime payments	23.6	8.6	16.7	5.2	2.4	3.0	12.2
incentive payments	12.4	7.4	10.1	8.8	1.6	3.2	7.8
shift premium payments etc.	5.6	1.9	3.9	2.4	1.8	1.9	3.2
Overtime, etc. as proportion of weekly wage (%)	25.5	8.0	16.0	16.2	4.3	6.4	13.6
Average total weekly hours, of which:	44.5	38.6	41.9	39.5	36.6	37.3	40.4
overtime hours	5.4	1.6	3.7	1.5	0.5	0.8	2.7

[1] Full-time employees on adult rates whose pay was not affected by absence.

Source: Adapted from Employment Gazette, Oct. 1985.

through the New Earnings Survey in April 1985. Clearly, differences in levels of pay are not the whole story. Manual workers must work far more hours than non-manual workers in order to achieve a given level of income.

2   Costs of work

Apart from the nature of the work itself, workplaces can be highly dangerous. Like so many other features of the work experience, the dangers are not evenly spread. Work-related accidents and disease are most prevalent among manual workers. Nearly all work deaths resulting from accidents at work are among *manual workers*. In the eighties there is evidence that deaths and injury at work are rising. In 1981 the number of fatal and major injuries (major fractures, amputations, eye injuries and accidents resulting in admittance to hospital as an in-patient for more than 24 hours) in British manufacturing stood at 4,193 according to the Health and Safety Executive (HSE). The figure rose to 4,709 in 1984, despite the marked decline in the numbers actually employed in manufacturing over the period. An increase of over 500 in the number of fatal and major injuries is certainly cause for some concern. Some people argue that it is a by-product of cutbacks in HM Factories Inspectorate, others that it is related to the wider economic recession (workers take chances rather than complain and lose their job). Either way, it is clear that conditions at work vary between occupational groups. In his monumental survey, *Poverty in the United Kingdom*, Professor **Peter Townsend** produced the following information about conditions at work in the late 1960s (see Table 7.4, p. 82).

Questions (Tables 7.3 and 7.4)

1. 'Over a quarter of male manual workers' weekly wage is derived from overtime and bonus payments.' True or false? What are the wider implications of reliance on overtime and bonuses in times of economic recession?
2 'The workplace has traditionally been divided into two camps: the blue- versus the white-collar worker.' How far does the evidence on contemporary rewards and conditions of work support this?
3 'Women are no nearer equality with men in terms of pay than

Table 7.4 Conditions of work, 1968–69 (percentage)

	Never at work before 8 a.m or at night	Pay does not fluctuate	Meals are subsidised	Occupational pension	Salary or wages paid during sickness	Unemployed more than 2 weeks in last year
Professional	85	74	53	90	97	0
Managerial	81	65	51	98	94	0
Supervisory (higher)	85	66	27	82	89	2
Supervisory (lower)	80	64	26	79	86	5
Routine non-manual	81	52	16	64	78	5
Skilled manual	54	38	18	46	53	4
Semi-skilled manual	50	36	23	51	50	6
Other manual	45	40	19	24	37	16

Source: Derived from P. Townsend, *Poverty in the United Kingdom*, Penguin Books, 1979.

they were ten years ago.' How could evidence in Tables 7.2 and 7.3 help to explain women's employment patterns and rewards?

The social construction of official labour statistics: unemployment and strikes

Sociologists are often reliant on official statistics for data on employment matters, but it is important to remember that such information is collected by official agencies for *administrative* purposes, quite different from those which a sociologist might have in mind. Statistics are collected in order to assist with specific government policies and objectives, not particular sociological research problems. As Richard Hyman states: 'A substantial gap in official provision is the almost total neglect of the *labour process*: the researcher who wishes to document developments in the rate of exploitation, or the intensification of labour, for example, will find little satisfaction from the official statistics' (from: 'Labour statistics', in J. Irvine, I. Miles and J. Evans (eds), *Demystifying Social Statistics*, Pluto Press, 1979, p. 235). Perhaps most important, it is necessary to recognise that statistical data – 'the facts' – are not so much discovered as *produced*, through series of elaborate procedures involving questions being posed and answers recorded in certain ways. The examples of statistics concerning unemployment and industrial relations are useful for demonstrating the 'social construction' of reality through official statistics.

1 Unemployment

The principal defect, from a sociological point of view, underlying official statistics on unemployment used to be that they covered only those people who were registered for work at the local Job Centres. During the 1970s various official and unofficial studies indicated that many potential workers failed to register, either because they were not entitled to benefit or because they did not wish to claim it, and hence were not recorded as unemployed. The most obvious group that this affected was married women. As **Deirdre Sanders** and **Jane Reed** recount:

In 1976, when official unemployment was around 1,350,000, of whom roughly one million were men, we conducted a

Fig. 7.1   The half-million gap

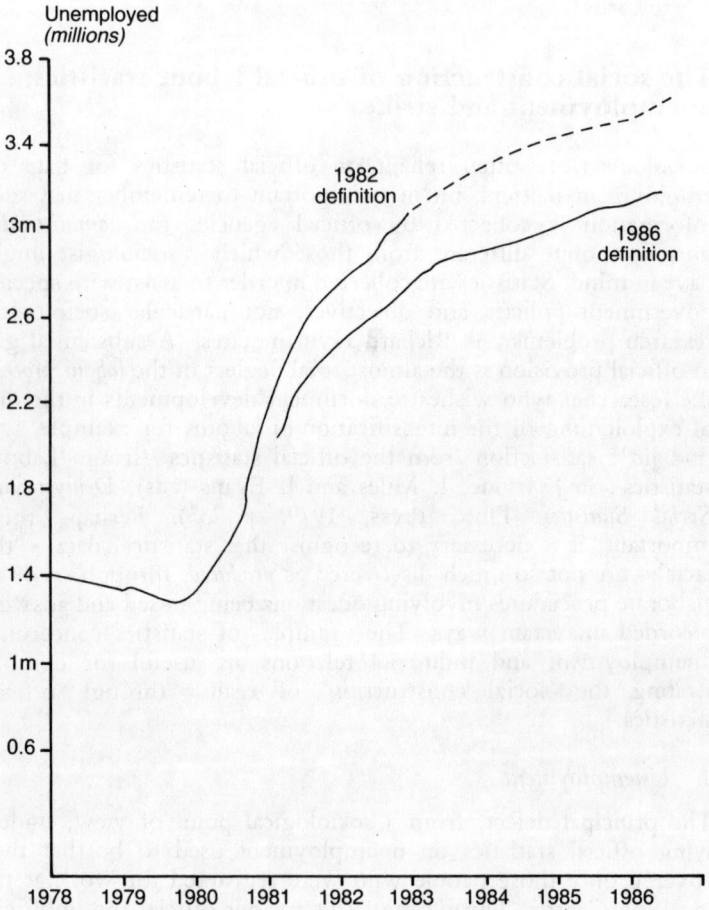

Note: Solid lines show official unemployment figures on the old basis (up to October 1982) and on the latest basis (since April 1986) but recalculated back to 1981). The broken line shows the Unemployment Unit estimate of the figures since October 1982 on the old basis.
Source: *New Statesman* 1 Aug. 1986, p. 8.

survey through *Women's Own* magazine and found that there were then 750,000 unregistered unemployed women – which took the nation's total to more than two million out of work. . . . The then Labour government were no keener officially to acknowledge the 'real' total than is the Conservative government today.

(From *Kitchen Sink or Swim?*, Penguin Books, 1982)

Since 1979, however, sixteen changes have been made in the unemployment count. Each one might be thought sensible and justifiable on its own, but as every one of these changes has been in a downward direction, the Thatcher administration has come under increasing criticism for 'massaging' the figures. Sociologically speaking, the changes have done nothing to improve the situation as it existed in the 1970s; indeed, since October 1982 the official figures have been less a record of unemployment than of benefit claimants who are looking for work. Figure 7.1 shows the difference between the new official figure and that calculated on the old basis before October 1982.

2 Strikes

If unemployment figures are currently the most carefully scrutinised official statistics, the second category most closely examined are probably those dealing with industrial stoppages. Information is derived from local Unemployment Benefit Office managers' reports, supplemented by examination of the press and by reports from employers. The main information published covers the number of disputes, workers 'directly' and 'indirectly' involved at affected establishments and 'working days lost'. Richard Hyman has listed three main defects with official strike statistics:

Some stoppages are simply not reported (the parties involved are under no obligation to do so) and fail to attract official attention. Disputes lasting less than a whole day, or involving less than ten workers, are excluded, unless the total of 'working days lost' exceeds 100. And only disputes relating to terms and conditions of employment are included; thus a number of important stoppages . . . do not appear in the statistics.

(R. Hyman in J. Irvine *et al.* (eds), *Demystifying Social Statistics*, p. 231)

Stoppage figures for 1984 therefore excluded disputes of a political nature, such as protests staged against government plans to abolish the Greater London Council and the Metropolitan County Councils. Additionally, there are difficulties: (a) deciding whether a particular episode should count as a strike (or 'lock-out', the official data do not differentiate); and (b) counting the precise numbers involved, or the time of the beginning and ending of a dispute. Hence the phrase 'working days lost' – there were 6,402,000 in 1985 – can be seen as misleading in so far as workers involved in a stoppage might otherwise be laid off because of production problems or shortages of orders. The simple point is that facts do not speak for themselves. Sociological interest is often in how official data are interpreted and presented to the public, via the press and broadcasting media. The extract from *Today* is an example of the social construction of the reality of industrial relations (see Fig. 7.2).

Questions

1 What would be a sociologically adequate definition of unemployment? How would it be measured?
2 Refer to the newspaper article:
   (a) What 'facts' support the headline?
   (b) What other factors might a sociologist want to know about before drawing this conclusion?
   (c) 'Unemployment levels have also made workers more reluctant to risk their jobs.' Discuss.

The household division of labour

Table 7.5 on p. 89 shows the results of an independent, nation-wide survey of attitudes towards the household division of labour.

Questions (Table 7.5)

1 In both categories, which tasks are (a) men, and (b) women most likely to do? Who has responsibility for routine household tasks?
2 What differences exist between what married people think

Fig. 7.2   An example of the social construction of industrial relations

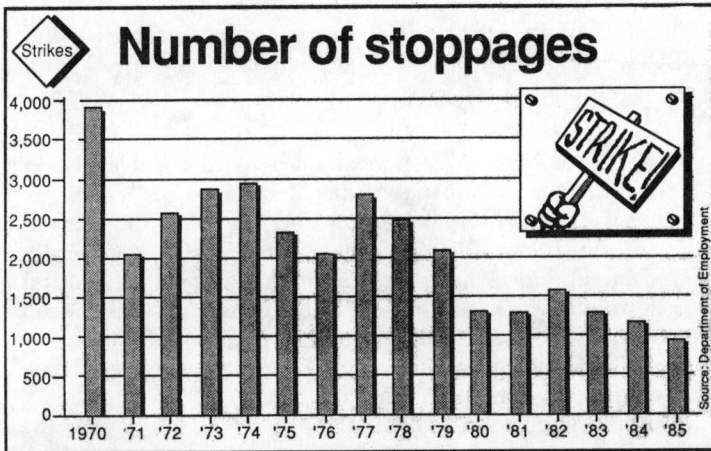

Number of stoppages

(Strikes)

4,000 —
3,500 —
3,000 —
2,500 —
2,000 —
1,500 —
1,000 —
500 —
0 —

1970 '71 '72 '73 '74 '75 '76 '77 '78 '79 '80 '81 '82 '83 '84 '85

Source: Department of Employment

Britain finds shopfloor harmony

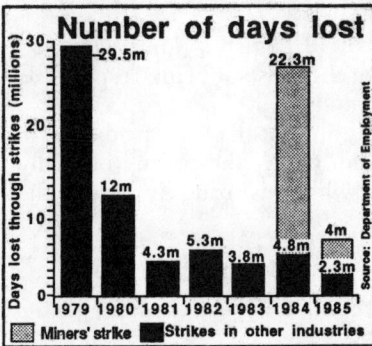

Number of days lost

30 —   –29.5m   22.3m
20 —
      12m
10 —   4m
         4.3m 5.3m 3.8m   4.8m
                                    2.3m
0 —
   1979 1980 1981 1982 1983 1984 1985

Days lost through strikes (millions)

Source: Department of Employment

▨ Miners' strike   ■ Strikes in other industries

BRITISH workers have rejected militancy and brought the rate of strikes down to its lowest for nearly 50 years.

New-found harmony on the shopfloor reduced stoppages in 1985 to 903, compared to 1,221 the previous year and 2,332 in 1975.

The total is the lowest since 1938, which had 885 stoppages.

Employment Department figures show the number of working days lost fell dramatically if the massive effect of the miners' strike is excluded.

The 1985 figure was

**by NEIL MAINLAND
Industrial
Correspondent**

6.3 million days, but the pit dispute accounted for 4 million. Without it, the number would have been the lowest since 1967.

One likely explanation for the change is the government's employment legislation making secret pre-strike ballots compulsory. Unemployment levels have also made workers more reluctant to risk their jobs.

The available labour force was 26.6 million in mid-1985, 192,000 more than the previous year.

Source: *Today*, 8 Aug. 1986

Fig. 7.3 Sexism in official statistics

The following extract illustrates a further problem with official labour statistics – the systematic exclusion of work *outside* employment.

So far as the production of statistics on work is concerned, sexism is evident on a number of levels. In the first place, through the definition of 'work' as meaning 'paid employment' and through the further concept of an 'economically active' or 'economically inactive' individual, the important domain of unpaid domestic work is omitted. Information on the unpaid domestic workforce of the country is simply not officially available. (In part this is, of course, because the state would have no use for such data.) Yet independent studies indicate the following:

1   that women contribute a substantially greater amount of domestic labour than men to the maintenance of households and the physical welfare of household members;

2   that about 85 per cent of all British women aged 16–64 years are 'housewives' in the sense of being responsible for the running of a household;

3   that 'housewives' who do not have a paid job in addition to their household work put in an (officially invisible) working week which is roughly twice the average industrial working week;

4   that those who perform the two kinds of work, housework and paid employment work, carry a double burden of which by definition only half appears in the official statistics relating to work.

(Ann and Robin Oakley, 'Sexism in official statistics', in J. Irvine *et al.* (eds), *Demystifying Social Statistics*, pp. 180–1)

Table 7.5   *Household division of labour: by marital status, Great Britain* (percentages)

| | Married respondents[1] | | | | | | Never married respondents[2] | | |
| | Actual allocation of tasks | | | Task should be allocated to | | | Tasks should be allocated to | | |
	Mainly men	Mainly women	Shared equally	Mainly men	Mainly women	Shared equally	Mainly men	Mainly women	Shared equally
Household tasks (percentage[3] allocation)									
Washing and ironing	1	88	9	—	77	21	—	68	30
Preparing evening meal	5	77	16	1	61	35	1	49	49
Household cleaning	3	72	23	—	51	45	1	42	56
Household shopping	6	54	39	—	35	62	—	31	68
Evening dishes	18	37	41	12	21	64	13	15	71
Organising household money and bills	32	38	28	23	15	58	19	16	63
Repairs of household equipment	83	6	8	79	2	17	74	—	24
Child-rearing (percentage[3] allocation)									
Looks after the children when they are sick	1	63	35	—	49	47	—	48	50
Teaches the children discipline	10	12	77	12	5	80	16	4	80

[1] 1,120 married respondents, except for the questions on actual allocation of child-rearing tasks which were answered by 479 respondents with children under 16.

[2] 283 never married respondents. The table excludes results of the formerly married (widowed, divorced or separated) respondents.

[3] 'Don't knows' and non-response to the question mean that some categories do not sum to 100 per cent.

Source: British Social Attitudes Survey, 1984, SCPR

should happen and what actually happens? Are these important?

3 'The stereotypical view of work in sociology, being what the husband does between the time he leaves his wife in the morning to when he returns in the evening has to be amended.' Discuss.

8 Documentary readings

The extracts presented here aim to highlight some of the themes and issues introduced in previous chapters. They are bunched into four areas: theory; skill and technology; unemployment and the work ethic; and contemporary trends and the future of work. Each area is accompanied by questions, discussion ideas and exercises.

Theory

As discussed in chapters 3 and 4, the sociological study of work has undergone a distinctive change in the past fifteen years. Prior to the publication of Harry Braverman's *Labor and Monopoly Capital*, industrial sociology tended to focus on worker attitudes, the origins and consequences of attitudes and 'orientations to work' (that is, the influence of non-work situations on worker attitudes to work and conceptions of social class). Since 1974, post-Braverman research has focused on such questions as the origins of work forms, management styles and strategies and control systems. In *The Nature of Work*, Paul Thompson looked at five post-Braverman themes: the reaction to Braverman's book; the deskilling debate; control and worker resistance; legitimation and consent; and the sexual division of labour. Thompson's book is the best introduction to debates on the 'labour process', and it also contains a useful glossary of labour process terms, extracts from which comprise the first reading.

Reading 8.1   Some labour process terms

alienated work   Work performed under conditions in which the worker is estranged from his or her own activity in the act of production, through the sale of labour power and the subordination of skills and knowledge to the capitalist, or other external social forces.

automation   A form of production in which all manual inter-vention by the worker is eliminated, in some cases to be replaced by supervision, monitoring or control of machinery. It includes a number of types such as continuous' process, numerical control and automated assembly; and it is distinguished from *mechanisation*, which concerns the operation of tools or machinery through sources independent of the worker's manual dexterity.

control system   Mechanisms by which employers direct work tasks, discipline and reward workers, and supervise and eval-uate their performance in production. See also *subordination of labour*.

deskilling   Incorporation of the crafts, knowledgeable practices and elements of job control held by workers into the functions of management, or operation of machinery.

division of labour   This is not the existence of different jobs, but the simplifying and fragmentation of tasks into smaller parts, so as to cheapen and control the costs of labour. Marx also uses a distinction between this *technical* division and the *social* divi-sion of labour, related to wider societal processes through which workers are allocated to different branches of production. This has relevance to the analysis of relations between social hierarchies of race and sex, and hierarchies in work.

forces and relations of production   A distinction between skills, machinery and other physical properties of production, and the social relations of ownership, command and control. These are held by Marx to act constantly on one another, enabling a critique to be made of those who believe that science and tech-nology are neutral.

Fordism   A term used by some labour-process theorists which extends the technique of factory production – based on the assembly-line – developed by Ford into a category referring to a general stage in capitalist production.

job enrichment   One form of work humanisation by employers. It is often used as a generic description of a number of different processes of enlarging, aggregating and rotating tasks.

labour power   The capacity to work which is transformed into *labour* that produces value for the capitalist through the creation of commodities.

labour process   The means by which raw materials are transformed by human labour, acting on the objects with tools and machinery – first into products for use and, under capitalism, into commodities to be exchanged on the market.

subordination of labour   Marx used these terms in a more precise way than that of *control*. The *formal* subordination of labour is established when workers and their skills are subsumed in a labour process under the control of the capitalist. This is ultimately transformed into *real* subordination through the incorporation of science and machinery within the expanded scale of production – which, in turn, allows a qualitatively new and more effective means of domination of labour.

worker resistance   A widely used term by labour process writers to refer to informal *and* organised worker opposition to management and employers in the labour process. It is more specific to work than the often misleading application of the concept of 'class struggle'.

(P. Thompson, *The Nature of Work*, Macmillan, 1983, pp. xiii–xvi)

Note: Make a note of any terms which you do not understand in the following extracts (and throughout this book). Look them up in one of the sociology dictionaries and keep a word list of your own, for future reference.

Reading 8.2   Job versus gender models in the sociology of work

Braverman's book was welcomed by feminists since it did, at least, recognise that 'the working class has two sexes'. However, much research in the sociology of work has often either utilised a 'unisex' theory or model of the social world (that what is the case for male workers, who are researched, will more or less apply to women) or treated women's employment as atypical or as secondary to their 'real' roles of mother and housewife. In the following extract Roslyn Feldberg and Evelyn Glenn discuss the assumptions of the 'two sociologies' of work: the job model for men and the gender model for women.

The sociology of work is essentially the study of how work connects individuals to the social structure . . . The most common topic for investigation is workers' response to work. However, the assumption underlying the explanations encompass not only the work setting, but also the basic connections of individuals to the larger social structure. These assumptions are different for men and women.

For men, it is assumed that economic activities provide the basis for social relationships within the family and in the society generally. For women, it is assumed that family care-taking activities determine social relationships. These different spheres of activity are, in turn, assumed to be combined in a nuclear family through the sexual division of labour – that is, man as economic provider and woman as wife and mother. Furthermore, male–female differences in relation to the family are expected to lead to differences in the nature of men's and women's connections to other parts of the social structure. For example, social class is assumed to be determined by economic position (i.e., relation to means of production, occupation) for the male, and by position in the family (i.e., wife, daughter) for the female. Similarly, the work attitudes and behaviour of men are seen as consequences of occupational experiences (for example, conditions of employment or occupational socializ-ation), while the responses of women are viewed as outcomes of family experiences (for example, household burden, femi-nine socialization). The major assumptions are set out in Table 8.1.

Questions

1 What evidence is there that 'man as economic provider and woman as wife and mother' are inaccurate descriptions of contemporary patterns of the sexual division of labour?

2 *Essay*: 'The ideology of housework/domesticity and women's place within the home has a material impact on women's paid work which in turn serves to reinforce that very ideology.' How has research in the sociology of work also served to re-inforce this ideology, according to Feldberg and Glenn?

Skill and technology

The next two extracts are from research carried out by Cynthia Cockburn into the relationships between men, women, skill and technological change. She explores the social processes involved in the introduction and use of new technology and thus develops, in a critical fashion, the post-Braverman debate on deskilling.

Table 8.1 Assumptions of the job model and the gender model

Assumptions	Job model	Gender model
Basic social relationships determined by:	Work	Family
Family structure is:	Male-headed, nuclear	Male-headed, nuclear
Connection to family is:	As economic provider/worker	As wife/mother
Social position determined by:	Work	Family
Socio-political behaviour and attitudes derived from:	Occupational socialization, class/status of occupation, social relations of work	Gender role socialization, family roles, activities and relationships of household work
Central life interest is in:	Employment and/or earnings	Family

(R. Feldberg and E.N. Glenn, 'Male and female: job versus gender models in the sociology of work', in J. Siltanen and M. Stanworth (eds), *Women and the Public Sphere*, Hitchinson, 1984, pp. 24–6)

Skill and deskilling

In the late 1970s Cockburn undertook research into the print workers in Fleet Street. In particular she focused on the feelings of male newspaper compositors to changes in their labour process brought about by the shift to computerised photocomposition. First, this entailed the abandonment of the 90 keyboard linotype machine and its replacement by the normal typewriter ('QWERTY-lay') keyboard in photosetting. Secondly, it marked a move away from the use of lead to the more familiar materials of paper, card and paste. In the following extract Cockburn explores the different meanings underlying the notion of 'deskilling'.

Reading 8.3   The nature of skill: the case of the printers

It is interesting to consider Harry Braverman's account of change in capitalist labour processes more generally, in the light of the experience in the printing industry. He took up and developed Marx's proposition that the more and more effective control of production by the capitalist class must lead to an ever-increasing division of labour and 'degradation' of work. Braverman defined as the first principle of scientific management, 'the dissociation of the labour process from the skills of workers'. The labour process is to be rendered independent of craft, tradition and workers' knowledge. Henceforth it is to depend not at all upon the abilities of workers but entirely upon the practices of management. . . . The recent experience of compositors points to a greater complexity than these theories allow. . . . *Skill* itself (if we read the men's experience in the hot metal aright) consists in at least three things. There is the skill that resides in the man himself, accumulated over time. . . . There is the skill demanded by the job – which may or may not match the skill in the worker. And there is the political definition of skill: that which a group of workers or a trade union can successfully defend against the challenge of employers and of other groups of workers. . . . is the loss of skill equivalent to the 'degradation of work'? Degradation can be measured along numerous scales; earnings, hours, conditions, the extent of the division of labour. In all these respects, newspaper workers, while being deskilled, have improved their lot throughout the fifties, sixties and seventies. For most, the change to new technology has brought a marked increase in earnings, a reduction in working hours, and a relaxation of pressure. . . . There is, however, one way in which the men *have* experienced degradation, and this accounts in part for their bitterness. Degradation can also be measured *socially*. Does the new work reduce the standing of the old worker relative to others in the working class? Because the work is more generalised and easier, the men feel they are slipping perilously down the worker scale toward the general 'hand' or labourer: 'I think I have gone from skilled to semi-skilled. . . .' 'It's just a kind of clerical job really. You couldn't call it print . . .' A further consideration is this. It is clear from the instance of photocomposition that the deskilling of one group of workers, and an overall weakening of the position of labour in society as a whole, may be achieved without actually deskilling the overall production process within the enterprise. . . . If capital gets its way, the composing group as a whole will be destroyed, and unemployment and loss of opportunities will occur at the societal level. yet, for those who remain in the slimmed-down newspaper, the massive routine copy-typing or 'input-tapping' job, characteristic of phase one of the new technology, will no longer exist as such. 'Typing' on the new keyboards will be a smaller (and more interesting) part of what are essentially other jobs – a part of the work-time of the journalist, editor, graphics person, or telephone answerer. . . . The question we are led to ask, then, is 'Is deskilling commensurate with loss of control?' . . . [In Braverman's] scenario, relentless deskilling dooms us to ever-diminishing control of work. But compositors have bought time in which some of them àt least may build up their competence and know-how on the new equipment in order to re-establish a degree of control. . . . Of course there are pressures pushing the other way. Electronic information technology is essentially a generalised technology applicable in all industries and throughout society. The comps' protected corner in the labour market is gone.

(C. Cockburn, *Brothers: Male Dominance and Technological Change*, Pluto Press, 1983, pp. 112–21)

Reading 8.4   New technology and gender

Cynthia Cockburn's most recent research project has looked at 'Advanced technology: effects on sex-gender and class relations in work'. In three case studies of operator jobs with new technology held by women – pattern making, in the clothing industry, a mail-order firm, and an X-ray department in a hospital – she found, both in terms of skill and control over work, that the jobs varied from good to very bad. But three characteristics were common to them all. First, the women involved reported increased pressure at work as employers sought to maximise the use of costly equipment; secondly, they felt vulnerable to technological change; and thirdly, they were not given any technical knowledge about the structure of the new equipment they were using.

Some relatively well-paid, secure and adaptable jobs which were created by the introduction of the new technology – such as maintenance technicians and systems technologists – were not taken by women. And upstream in the engineering industry, where the technologies originated, women were not entering these jobs either. In a firm producing 'computerised tomography' (C.T.) scanners for hospital X-ray departments, Cockburn found, 'of 197 technical managers and engineers/engineering technicians . . . *none* was female. Twenty-two out of the 23 software engineers (a desk job) were men.' Cockburn wanted to find out why this was the case. She believed that discrimination against women was likely to be one answer, but additionally, and more subtly, that what she calls *power relations of sex and gender* actively structure the relations between men, women and technology. Interviews with male technologists and technicians revealed that they favoured and developed friendships through

> the mutual exchange of knowledge and a humorous competi-tiveness concerning technology. A great deal of their enjoy-ment of work derives from this style of relationship with colleagues and clients. Men continually define women as *not* technological. By this dual process they create a highly mascu-line-gendered social environment and a woman cannot fit into it. Women are aware of the discomfort that would be involved for them in attempting to enter technological work and, in a sense, boycott it.

After .conducting follow-up interviews, Cockburn concluded that the evidence

> points to an appropriation of the technological sphere by men – both in a material way with material effects, and ideologi-cally. . . . Technological competence correlates strongly with masculinity and incompetence with feminity. Women who have attempted to enter the male technical sphere of work, or even to take up 'do-it-yourself' and technical hobbies, say they have to make an impoverishing choice: they may be competent but unfeminine (and therefore unlovable); or they may be feminine but by definition incompetent.

In sum, Cockburn argues that to understand the continuing technological job segregation by sex it is necessary to have a concept of long-term, organised male self-interest, and of systematic male dominance – or patriarchy. In the study of work and technological change there are two sets of interrelated relations which need to be recognised:

> On the one hand, capital applies new technologies to class advantage, 'revolutionizing the forces of production' with the effect of wresting back control of production from skilled workers, increasing productivity and maximising profit. On the other hand, men *as men* appropriate and sequester the technological sphere, extending their tenure (not control – that remains with capital) over each new phase, at the expense of women.

> (C. Cockburn, 'The relations of technology', in R. Crompton and M. Mann (eds), *Gender and Stratification*, Polity Press, 1986)

Questions

1 What is meant by 'the dissociation of the labour process from the skill of workers'?

2 How do you think Cockburn would explain the Wapping dispute involving Rupert Murdoch's News International and the printworkers' unions?

3 What does Cockburn mean when she writes that 'power relations of sex and gender' structure the relations between men, women and technology?

4 Debate the pros and cons of new technology for (a) employers, (b) workers, (c) men, (d) women.

5 *Essay* (linked to Chapters 3 and 4): 'Whatever sympathy one might have with Braverman's more general "deskilling" thesis, it has to be recognised that the "office proletariat" is not a mass, but stratified by age, qualifications, and, most importantly, gender' (R. Crompton and G. Jones, 1984). Discuss.

Reading 8.5 *Unemployment and the work ethic*

The extract in this section is taken from *Unemployment: Its Social Psychological Effects* by Peter Kelvin and Joanna Jarrett. The authors are critical of many of the assumptions held by 'public opinion' and social scientists about unemployment. In particular they cite the concept of the 'Protestant work ethic' which was originally a highly academic, and idealistic, notion. But recently it has been used to explain attitudes to work, unemployment and the unemployed. As academics and journalists have treated it as a self-evident truth it has become a part of 'public opinion', accepted by the unemployed themselves. Kelvin and Jarrett continually evaluate the notion in the following extract, thus demonstrating the need for social scientists to be on their guard against prevailing ideologies in contemporary society.

When one explores the evidence, it becomes very doubtful indeed whether there is a cultural norm of a Work Ethic, Protestant or otherwise. It is even more doubtful if there ever was such a norm. . . . the essential facts seem to be these. The sixteenth and especially the seventeenth centuries saw the economic rise of a *section* of the middle class which was genuinely inspired by a sense of the religious significance of work, and of frugality in their personal lives – what Weber called 'asceticism': and so the profits from work were not to be used to indulge in luxuries, or to retire from work, but to create more work, and thereby more opportunities for serving God. . . . these values and sentiments were never more than those of a minority, and of middle-class rather than working- or upper-class origin. The notion that the generality of English workers were imbued with this Ethic just does not survive examination. For at least the last five hundred years, there is steady and consistent evidence of late coming to work, long breaks at work, early leaving of work, downing of tools at the first opportunity, and the like disdain for work (Kelvin, 1984). To take one example: in the 1860s, at the height of that reputedly so marvellously industrious Victorian England, and at its very centre, Birmingham:

An enormous amount of time is lost, not only by want of punctuality in coming to work in the morning and the beginning again after meals, but still more by the general observation of 'St. Monday'. . . . One employer has on Monday only 40 or 50 out of 300 or 400. (Parliamentary Papers, 1884, cited Royston Pyke, 1967, p. 88).

. . . Furthermore, the English worker was typically not a church- or chapel-goer in what in any case had long not been the church- and chapel-going society of another popular myth. From at least the eighteenth century, the growth of the towns, and therefore the reduced surveillance of and social pressures on the individual, led to a fall in religious attendance which greatly worried non-conformists, as well as the established church. . . .

As for the 'masters', the predominant ideal amongst these was not that of the Protestant Work Ethic, but of the 'gentleman': the gentleman who perhaps tended his estates, who would be expected to cultivate worthwhile pursuits, but who would not, ideally, have to work at all. . . .

When one looks at the situation from the very historical perspective which ostensibly gave rise to it, explanations in terms of the Protestant Ethic emerge as little more than an invention of twentieth-century social science, with unwarranted pretensions to an ancient lineage. The 'ethic' which has truly been predominant and pervasive is not a work ethic but, for want of a better term, a *wealth ethic*. . . . The 'ethic' is to make or to have sufficient wealth not to have to depend on others; work is only one means to that end, and certainly not the one universally most esteemed: not in any class. Provided that one has money enough to be independent, there is no great moral obligation to work, certainly not in the sense of gainful, productive employment.

(P. Kelvin and J.E. Jarrett, *Unemployment: Its Social Psychological Effects*, Cambridge University Press, 1985, pp. 101–4)

Questions

1 Examine newspaper, radio and TV coverage of unemployment. Is the notion of a 'work ethic' in widespread use?

2 Can we do without the notion of a 'work ethic'?

3 *Essay/discussion*: 'We do not at this time have any clear basis on which we can make the crucially important distinction between the effects of unemployment and the effects of poverty which almost invariably goes with it' (Kelvin and Jarrett). Discuss.

Contemporary trends and the future of work

Aside from mass unemployment, the relocation of production and changes in the occupational structures, since the 1960s governmental bodies and academics have become interested in the (apparent) growth of the 'hidden' or 'black' economy. Estimates vary as to its size and there is debate over its significance. In the first extract here Philip Mattera, writing about the USA, suggests that it is a symptom of the general fragmentation of work, and a sign of people seeking freedom from commercial and bureaucratic conformity. Tony Watts, on the other hand, in the second extract, provides a more sober appraisal of 'informal economies' generally, and suggests that they have to be understood in connection with changes in the mainstream formal market economy, and wider communal and family relations.

Reading 8.6　Working off the books

A regular job is no longer one's primary activity, the basis of one's social identity. Rather it is often simply a means to qualify for unemployment compensation. . . . Some may bitterly resent the fact, but others have come to embrace it as part of a new 'lifestyle'. In fact, partial dependence on government benefits is yet another characteristic of the lives of the poor that has extended to much larger portions of the population. This is not to say that class differences or inequality in the distribution of income have disappeared; it simply means that a fragmented and precarious relationship to work and income has become more common throughout advanced capitalist societies. Just as the model of the nuclear family has come to represent only a small minority of US households, so the model of the full-time, permanent 'career' job is relevant to smaller and smaller numbers of workers. . . .

Instability and irregularity in employment, which was at the root of the marginalization of the ghetto populations of the US, is, in a different form, now a relatively desirable arrangement for many others. In some instances, the willingness to toil in such a way may be the only way for someone to qualify for a good regular job. . . .

We have come a long way from the classical Marxist labor

force consisting simply of those who are regularly employed and others in various forms of the reserve army. While the dynamics of the accumulation process that Marx uncovered have not disappeared entirely, the nature of wage-labor and unemployment has undergone some fundamental changes. The combined effect of expanded precarious work in regular jobs, wider use of government benefits, hustling, and the under-ground economy add up to something that looks very different from the traditional labor market. To the extent that capital uses the new arrangements to increase the degree of exploi-tation, the new situation is simply an erosion of the power of the workers. But insofar as people are able to turn the new forms of income-generating activity to their advantage, the structure is less of a *market* and more of a terrain in the struggle for some measure of social autonomy.

(P. Mattera, *Off the Books: the Rise of the Underground Economy*, Pluto Press, 1985, pp. 25–6)

Reading 8.7   *The informal economies*

The first is the '*black*' economy, otherwise variously known as the 'underground' or 'hidden' economy. This covers work conducted wholly or partly for money which is concealed from taxation and regulatory authorities: it ranges from undeclared criminal and immoral earnings (e.g. prostitution, drug-trafficking), through office pilfering and perks, to undeclared income earned in particular by the self-employed, by 'moon-lighters', and by the unemployed. . . .

The black economy is closely related to the formal economy, in the sense that it is still focused around a cash nexus. This is not however true of the other two informal economies. The first of these is the *communal* economy, which involves the production of goods or services that are consumed by people other than the producers, but are not sold on a monetary basis. This ranges from baby-sitting circles or car pools which operate on the basis of a formal exchange of tokens or credits, through exchanges of skills or of equipment which are part of a relationship of generalized reciprocity between friends, neigh-bours, etc., to pure gift activities for which no reciprocity is expected. . . .

The third informal economy is the *household* economy, which covers work within the home that involves the production for internal consumption of goods or services for which approximate substitutes might otherwise be purchased for money. These include cooking, decorating, laundry, child care, home repair, garden produce, etc. In the USA, Burns (1975) has estimated that if all the work carried out within the household by men and (particularly) women were converted into monetary form, the total would be equal to the entire amount paid out in wages and salaries by every corporation in the country. In Britain, Gershuny (1979) has calculated on the basis of time-budget figures that by 1974/5 the total time devoted to household production (i.e. domestic work) in the UK amounted to about four-fifths of that devoted to formal economic activities. . . .

It is important to emphasize that there is not much evidence of the unemployed moving in a substantial way into the informal economies. . . . In particular, it seems clear that the black economy is not significantly manned by the unemployed. Certainly some 'fiddling' goes on, but the Economist Intelligence Unit (1982) found in a survey of over 1,000 unemployed people that 61 per cent said they had done no casual work at all, and only 8 per cent said they had received payment of some kind. Broadly similar results were found by Roberts *et al.* (1981) in the case of young people: 'steady hustles' were more prevalent in neighbourhood gossip than in real life, and few of those involved in the black economy had discovered genuine long-term alternatives to orthodox employment.

(A.G. Watts, *Education, Unemployment and the Future of Work*, Open University Press, 1983, pp. 155–9)

Questions

1   Discuss, in small groups, the first sentence of Reading 8.6.
2   Under the headings 'black', 'communal' and 'household' list jobs carried out in each category according to Watts. Could these jobs be done in all economies (including the 'formal')? What is distinctive about jobs currently carried out in the household economy?

Reading 8.8   The future of work

Finally, A.G. Watts reminds us that the conception we have of the future of work rests ultimately upon judgements of *value* and hence is a political one:

The issues are basically five-fold:

1 What relative value do we attach to work and to leisure?
2 What relative value do we attach to paid work and to unpaid work?
3 What are the forms of work we are prepared to pay for?
4 How are these forms of work to be distributed?
5 How is this distribution to be related to the generation and distribution of wealth?

These are profound questions, and profoundly political ones. The answers to which we have become accustomed since the Industrial Revolution are arguably not going to work any more.

(A.G. Watts, *Education, Unemployment and the Future of Work*, Open University Press, 1983, pp. 174–5)

Questions

1 Discuss these questions in class.
2 How do different sociological perspectives on work answer these questions?

9 Projects and exercises

The following suggestions are made for enlivening the under-standing of certain issues and themes in the sociology of work.

1 Role play

This can be very useful for highlighting the 'negotiated order' of industrial relations. Students are allocated roles: (a) on a committee to discuss health and safety at work; (b) as representatives of management, government and trade unionists discussing pay and conditions. Role play of industrial relations can also highlight the *rule-governed* nature of such activity.

2 Media watch

Although strikes are not the only sign of industrial conflict and unease, they are widely covered in the media. In the 1970s reports in the press and on TV and radio often gave the impression that Britain was permanently beset by a major industrial stoppage. Yet Britain's strike record is not nearly so bad as is commonly supposed. One straightforward exercise is to collect different newspapers' accounts of a particular dispute. It may also be possible to record and monitor TV and radio accounts. Compare the content and styles of reporting in the 'quality' and the 'popular' newspapers (for example, *The Times*, *Guardian* and *Telegraph*, versus the *Star*, *Mirror* and *Sun*). What information is made available by the parties involved in the dispute, and how do they present their cases? Look at the language used in the reporting of the stoppage. Is it neutral, or 'loaded' in a certain way?

3 Time budgets

Time-budget surveys involve participants who keep a diary of their daily activities – recording every half-hour or so what they were doing – paid work, education, leisure (physical recreation, watching TV, listening to records/tapes, reading, walking and so on), cooking, cleaning or child-minding. Keep a record of the activities conducted by yourself and other members of your household through a week and/or over a weekend. Is there an equal share-out of routine, domestic duties? Who does what? What do people define as 'work'? Findings can be compared with others in your sociology class, and patterns discussed.

4 The local economy and labour market

Urban sociologists (such as R. Pahl *et al.*, *Structures and Processes of Urban Life*, Longman, 1983) argue that where you live and what particular industries are available to you influence the way in which economic recession and job losses are experienced. It is important therefore to find out about your local economy and labour market. Local authorities, such as the city council, can provide much useful and up-to-date information about trends in employment, unemployment, incomes, population changes and so on. Find out the chief industries and employers.

Is there much paid work available for women? If so, in which industries? It might be possible to trace the fortunes of your biggest local employer. When did it begin? What is the impact of recession upon it? For a splendid illustration of local labour market research, see Benwell Community Development Project, *The Making of the Ruling Class*, which is based on industrial changes in the North-east of England (available from Benwell CDP, 85–87 Adelaide Terrace, Benwell, Newcastle upon Tyne, NE4 8BB).

5 Personal accounts

An increasingly popular method of social historians and socio-logists is to seek personal accounts, or 'oral histories', of ordinary men and women. Such accounts can provide descriptive testi-monies of what really goes on inside factories, offices and the professions which would otherwise be unavailable to outsiders. You can start by interviewing an older relation or parent about their working life, or you might approach a neighbour who is retired or still working. For examples of personal accounts of work, see R. Fraser (ed.), *Work: Twenty Personal Accounts* (2 volumes, Penguin Books, 1968 and 1969); S. Terkel, *Working* (Penguin Books, 1977); and Television History Workshop, *Making Cars: A History of Car Making in Cowley*, Routledge & Kegan Paul, 1986. For some guidelines about recording individuals' accounts, see S. Humphries, *The Handbook of Oral History*, Inter-Action Inprint, 1984.

Further reading

The following books and resources are considered readable and of value for study and reference purposes on introductory courses. While all the sociology textbooks cover the subject of work, Lee and Newby give a good account of the neo-Durkheimian school. In contrast, the books by Hill and Thompson are neo-Weberian and neo-Marxist respectively. Brown's long essay ranges across a number of central issues and pieces of research data to produce an example of sociological writing at its very best. Dex provides a comprehensive discussion of the importance of gender divisions in analysing work, and Oakley's text is the classic source in Britain for treating housework *as work* within sociological research. Terkel provides individual accounts of work, while Littler has edited essays on the experience of work in different settings, not just formal industrial employment in the West. Hyman's book is now in its third edition and remains the most useful critical exploration of industrial conflict available. The two books edited by Forester cover the area of new technology in encyclopaedic fashion – from what it is to what it might become, and its social implications. Mattera's text considers work in the 'black economy' in international and comparative perspective. Ashton's book is the best overview of unemployment, while Roberts and Walker and Barton offer contrasting approaches to the study and understanding of its impact on young people. Finally Watts, Pahl, and Clarke and Critcher, in different ways, provide food for thought about the past, present and future of work.

Ashton, D. N., *Unemployment under Capitalism: the Sociology of British and American Labour Markets*, Wheatsheaf Books, 1986.
Brown, R. 'Work', in Abrams P. and Brown, R. (eds), *UK Society*, Weidenfeld and Nicolson, 1984.
Clarke, J. and Critcher C., *The Devil Makes Work: Leisure in Capitalist Britain*, Macmillan, 1985.
Dex, S., *The Sexual Division of Work*, Wheatsheaf Books, 1985.

Forester T. (ed.), *The Microelectronic Revolution*, Basil Blackwell, 1980.

———, *The Information Technology Revolution* Basil Blackwell, 1985.

Hill, S., *Competition and Control at Work*, Heinemann, 1981.

Hyman, R., *Strikes*, Fontana, (3rd edition) 1984.

Lee, D. and Newby, H., *The Problem of Sociology*, Hutchinson, 1983.

Littler, C. (ed.), *The Experience of Work*, Gower, 1985.

Mattera, P., *Off the Books – the Rise of the Underground Economy*, Pluto Press, 1985.

Oakley, A., *The Sociology of Housework*, Martin Robertson, 1985.

Pahl, R., *Divisions of Labour*, Basil Blackwell, 1984.

Roberts, K., *School Leavers and Their Prospects: Youth and the Labour Market in the 1980s*, Open University Press, 1984.

Terkel, S., *Working*, Penguin, 1977.

Thompson, P., *The Nature of Work: Introduction to Debates on the Labour Process*, Macmillan, 1983.

Walker, S. and Barton L. (eds), *Youth, Unemployment and Schooling*, Open University Press, 1986.

Watts, A. G. *Education, Unemployment and the Future of Work*, Open University Press, 1983.

Index